HANDICAP AND LOVING IT

By

Eddie Burley

ISBN: 0-75962-904-8

This book is printed on acid free paper.

1stBooks - rev. 07/09/01

TABLE OF CONTENTS

INTRODUCTION
A TOWN NEAR YOU

I know darn well that you know me. You've seen my work everywhere. But where ever I go you try and turn your head as though I'm not there. My work is powerful and formidable. There may be a few similarities involved each time you see me but my work is unmistakably an one of a kind. In your own little defiant way you refuse to acknowledge me. And because you will not recognized me you tend not to accept me. Do you actually believe that if you stick your head in the ground and close your eyes that I'll go away. Remember this, I'm as old as life itself. You may not remember me and maybe you just don't want to remember me. To some of you, you may even know me by another name. You see it for yourself. I'm not going anywhere and there is nothing that you can do about it either. My numbers are steadily increasing and I'm getting stronger and more powerful everyday. It really bothers me when you set there and try to ignore me. It's a sign of disrespect. What, you think that you're too good for me or something? You think that you can treat me any kind of a way?

Well, think on this for a while. You know that beautiful bombshell of a woman, the one with the body figure so fine that she could have been hand molded from every man's imagination at the same time. And the lovely soft skin that's so delicate to the touch that waving your hands through the clouds would not even be a comparison. Then you rub your fingers through her hair and feel the silkiness that would be the envy of any worm. When you look into her eyes you can see the heavens and the beginning of life. And the only thing in life that she would ever ask for is to be with you and only you. You could just die to be with this woman. Or either she don't exist and if she did it would only be there in a dream. She might even be the one that you drool over in those girlie magazines. Or she could be sitting in the room across the floor, the one that everyone gaze's at from a distance but will never say anything to.

I've seen her. I can get her. I even may already have her. I can get her even if she is only a figment of your imagination. Now, who am I?

And you, Mr. Big time Corporate Executive, living the life of Riley, you think that you've got it made. With all those major decisions you must make and the glory of big money and leer jets, your work is nothing compared to mine. With all the power that you might posses my work can render yours absolutely useless.

That unborn baby that you're carrying in your womb is not beyond my reach. I can do my work even to those who haven't got here yet. Yeah, I know that may sound a little harsh to you but that's just the way I operate.

My work is done in the ghetto's and slums all around the world. I can do it from a basketball court or a drive-by shooting or just riding on a bicycle.

It makes no difference to me if you're young or old, man, woman, black or white. I demand more attention than I'm getting. Your stubborn refusal to appreciate me or understand me is only going to make my numbers grow larger until you're forced to the point that you'll have to deal with me. Then you'll know my true power.

I am ruthless. I am cunning. I am without mercy or sorrow. I am deliberate and non-discriminating. Once you've seen my work up close I'll have you praying to God to have me removed. I feature a cast of characters that you may not understand but have very well come to know. They are: blindness, multiple-sclerosis, diabetes, polio, paralysis and brain damage, just to name a few. Sure, now you recognize me, I am disability and I'm coming to a town near you.

PREFACE

STOP AND SMELL THE COFFEE

One of the biggest loves of my life has always been my ability to use and create things with my hands and my mind. This ability has played a vital role in my life as far as I can remember and was a determining factor in my chose of career opportunities.

My childhood years were consumed with taking apart my toys to find out how they worked and then reassembling them in a workable fashion of my own.

I turned to music, then learned to play the trumpet and became a member of the David T. Howard Marching Rams Band, a honor that I am very proud of. This talent provided importance because it brought me a music scholarship to the elite Morris Brown Wolverines Marching 100, where I attend college.

My interest expanded to art, where as, I must say so myself, I was pretty darn good, making sculptures and paintings that were awed and admired by quiet a few. The money however, sucks. It's hard to make a living that way because you have to be dead before your work becomes famous. I think that's why artist are referred to as 'starving'.

So as it would be, mechanical engineering turned out to be a perfect fit for me since it gave me the opportunity to work with my hands, it required a lot of use of my mental abilities, and it allowed plenty of room for growth and creativity. The art of it is the way I honed my skills and the way I masterfully displayed my abilities and craftsmanship.

I was at a phase in my life where everything seemed to be coming together. All obstacles and challenges had already been hurdled. My job and lifestyle had all come together and all that was left was to settle down reaching that final plateau where everyone strides to be. Then suddenly, there's this accident where I was left in a state of quadriplegic.

During rehabilitation there were several consultations made with my doctors. One of them included the use of my hands. I understood from the beginning that they would be the last of my many lost functions to be restored. I understood that and accepted it well, but.

At the clinic part of the recovery process includes recreational therapy. The intent is to try and keep your mind occupied as not to dwell too much on your condition. The idea thrilled me and would give me the chance to once again display my creative talents. My decision was to make a bowl out of clay. I became depressed and a tear formed in my eye when I found out that I was no longer able to be creative because of my hands. So I left that session.

My spirit was broken as a person and my feelings became that of being a totally useless being. It was a very hard mental and emotional battle within me trying to convince myself to carry on and then wondering why even try.

This is without a doubt the most dramatic change to endure. Life becomes meaningless, faith is questioned and the future does not exist. One more hurdle in life.

With this book I wish to once again be able to artistically display my creative abilities by bringing back the human side of a physically challenged person.

So often people with challenges are rejected or withdrawn from society and become an almost forgotten person, just a statistical number. Immediately when people see a physically challenged person sympathy starts to pour out and if they are religious they began to count their blessings of how well they are off. Everything imaginable they think of a challenged person as far as their abilities or disabilities to do things as a quote "normal" unquote person.

Little do they know the advantages a challenge person has and once they realize it only then do they begin to understand who is really at the disadvantage. This in itself is the beginning of the advantages.

Being consider challenged is not always a birth defect, it is something that can happen to anyone at anytime. It has no prejudices. You could be riding a horse and fall off, driving your car home from work and be involved in an accident, or simply walking around the house in your own home and fall. This very well could be you.

In this effort I want to bring awareness to a broken and seemingly forgotten people in order to restore the pride, the dignity, and the financial independence that they need and deserve.

I want to take away that statistical number that society always categorize people with and give them back their face and their name. This book is intended to bring inspiration to disabled people all around the world.

This experience has given me the ability to reach into the bowels of death and pull out this book, an advantage that I would not have known if I had not been disabled.

Life is not so bad at all, just stop and smell the coffee, there's benefits to being handicap.

Eddie Burley

CHAPTER ONE
THE BENEFITS OF BEING HANDICAP

Snap!!!, the last sound I heard as my head hit the ground and in a sudden instant without a second thought I knew my neck was broken. This defining moment in time ended life as I had come to know and it was the first sound that I heard beginning the ride to a journey that could not have been imagined even with all my knowledge, travel and wisdom.

As my limp body lay motionless on the floor unable to respond to any commands from my mind, (such as, "get-up"), I called out to my wife, "Ethel, call 911, I think I broke my freaking neck." Shortly there afterwards the paramedics arrived and after a quick examination they said, "he broke his freaking neck." At this point the only thought that crossed my mind was "well, at least I don't have to go to work today and I have a good excuse." Life is good.

As we entered the hospital passing people with gunshot wounds, stabs, a few pregnancies and even a couple of people with gas from the chili they ate the night before, all the attention of the staff seemed to be centered around me. Then it hit me, something important was happening here.

There was a lot of excitement with paramedics, doctors and nurses scurrying around in a heated rush and beckoning to your every whimpering demand. It was like a conformation of the reality of that old cliché, 'I'm the man." Now here, vying for only my attention was "hundreds of thousands of dollars", of talents and equipment that ranks with perhaps the best in the world. The customer service satisfaction ratings would have been the envy of "Caesar's Palace" or the "Trump Tower's".

And the drugs, "ah man", some of the purist grade and highest quality stuff you've ever seen, not that I'd know anything about that, but all there's left to say is "ah man" the stuff is good.

There came a point when reality began to set in as your mind realizes that you're now off to a journey to a place you've never been before. The sooner you are willing to accept the fact that you are here rather than denying it is the key to victory as you are now free to utilize good energy in other areas, such as, honing new skills.

Once you have a grasp on how to utilize these new skills you begin to tingle as the power of control spew from your fingertips. If you don't like your service, the staff will modify it, change it or they'll improve it. If you want more of something, they'll give you more, etc., etc., etc.

I found myself in a situation where some of the things that most men can only dream about was now about to happen to me where in this next area surrounded by beautiful women of all shapes, sizes and colors my body was being violently attacked with the speed of piranha as an unwilling victim enters the forbidden zone. While my clothes were being torn away my whole body was being caressed and massaged in ways like never before by these visions of loveliness as I embark into my journey to the stairways of heaven.

This constant display of affection and bombardment for attention can easily become distracting and overwhelming but could only be equaled to the media hypes of being a Muhammad Ali or a Michael Jordan with the world "on-call" just to serve you.

Being sometimes in situations you dream for, hope for and even pray for only to find these situations are all so true, you ask yourself, "am I dreaming?" No, it's not a dream and yes it's very real. So by now you began murmuring to yourself "poor dumb sucker, in an ideal situation and can't do a thing about it." Well here's where reality sets in because all the 'macho men' and 'male chauvinist pigs' in good health could not perform under these conditions for fear of poor performance. That's why the best tales of sexual empowerment are often told involving one on one's and private sessions which leaves no witnesses to dispute one's testimony, and I'd be lying if I said that I wasn't enjoying all this attention.

Now that I have your attention, 'walk with me grasshopper'.

The next thing that you remember morning rises and you're awakened by the soft, sweet whisperings of a sexy songbird singing your name and nudging you gently. If you could play a little low volume "Hootie & the Blowfish" in the background your mind could easily start to wandering, this could be my wife or this used to be my wife, anyway, let's not loose the thought here. The heat of a strange woman's hand being laid on your chest as you're being prepared for bath and full body massage brings to memory times I'd sneak away from work to be with other folks wives, "Oh, what a feeling."

My breakfast is already prepared for me, with anything of my choosing, and spoon fed during intelligent morning conversation with my head resting comfortably on a fully developed pair of breast while cuddled in the arms of a total stranger. Moments such as these are truly valuable if you've by-passes the self pity and developed those new skills.

It's often been said that you can't see the forest for the trees and that is so true because one has the tendency to be so close to life and trying to improve the quality of life so much that they forget to live and appreciate how good they already have it. This morning for example, full schedule on my calendar, meetings, appointments, people over for dinner, the whole nine yards. And as faith would have it I'm running late (literally speaking); what a wonderful way to start a Monday. Business as usual?, quite the contrary, for you see this morning I now have the luxury of having my quarters cleaned and properly cared for while I'm away on other chores.

You've no idea how long the dreams of hitting the lottery or the one of a rich uncle dying and leaving behind large sums of cash can creep into your mind. Better yet, maybe, one day while walking down the street there will be a bag of money to be found, or one day I'll start my own business. Lets see, with just twenty more years of service on this job, maybe I can afford to be served at the age of 75. Not!!! Should there be difficulties arriving to destinations on time or keeping scheduled appointments, the services of a personal valet is of great value to have at your disposal. (And while you're at it, no starch in the shorts and fold the shirts.

This is only the beginning.

One of the more treasured events of the day is therapy. The torture and excruciating pain that is endured in these two hour personal sessions of massages and stretching is devastating enough to bring tears the strongest mans eyes. The mixture of therapist consist of ten year veterans and interns with an average in age of twenty-five years old. Needless to say, this is a very physical and demanding job requiring all types of positions and conditions, therefore, each person must dress accordingly, i.e., jeans, short pants, stretch pants, swim suits and almost always "T"-shirts. This is torturous enough just trying to talk about it. May we bow our heads for a moment of silence.

As this carnage continues the suffrage intensifies, being sometimes forced to watch the aerial assault of braless breast as they descend from the heavens above to strike yet another compromising position in their deliverance of therapy. Keep in mind this is not an all pleasure and no work event but due to the fact this is a medical situation, some side effects do exist. One being the weakened state of some muscle groups which requires assistance from another to help you obtain certain positions.

We are all limited in our range of motions that we share as humans, which, includes our therapist, thus, ultimately requiring other body parts as aides. Therefore, it is not unreasonable to find your head, chest or back being supported by a soft, cushiony, warm body part of a female persuasion. More times than can be remembered has the crotch been used to aide or support the arms, legs and even hands.

The second side effect is muscle spasms. Muscle spasms are involuntary reactions to muscle groups but can be controlled with drugs, exercise and time. Probably, the most important time ever to be encountered where full awareness of those wonderful new skills are deeply appreciated is now. A well timed properly placed involuntary muscle spasm can reap rewards of some of the best gifts Mother-nature can supply. Oh, the pain; I do love therapy so.

The skill levels of this staff is magnificent, almost angelic in the manner they carry out the performance of they're duties. Never before have I seen patients so energetic and enthusiastic to participate in a therapy session that requires work, pain and suffering and the staff seems to enjoy it just as much as the patients do.

The hidden factor to the entire element, though, is the psychological benefits bestowed upon one in a most stealth-like manner. Where it not for the fact that the results are so influential it could be very easy to become up-set at the deceit perpetrated during a time when pity and compassion would naturally seem to be the norm. Nobody loves you but your mama!

In no time at all a transformation from an unwilling victim to a willing activist has occurred with the guide of this fine group of people who force you deep into yourself to find out who you truly are.

Now a bond has been formed that will definitely withstand the test of time. Partnerships, marriages and siblings will falter before one link in this chain will ever begin to weaken. Relationships develop as personal stories are shared during periods of meeting and spending time with one anther's families. Personalities and animosities are checked at the door. It has the visual of an awful road to take, suppose to some it matters not how you get there as long as the results are the same; maybe the end does justify the means, never-the-less, here-in is found one of the things we all keep searching for... 'UNCONDITIONAL LOVE.'

CHAPTER TWO
OUT ON A STROLL

Morning had arrived and the rays of sunshine began to pierce through the window as Bob opened the entry door to gather in the daily paper. The sweet music being offered by the local songbirds offered a refreshing refrain to the brisk morning air. Fallen leaves swirled around in a small whirlwind near the corner of the stairs as if dancing to the chirping sounds from above. It was a beautiful morning and the first day of fall, his favorite time of the year and such a wonderful time to be outside.

While enjoying another cup of coffee from his special coffee cup he shared a few minutes on the porch and cheered to the serenade being performed at his door. It seemed such a waste to loose time as precious as this so he hurried back inside in preparations to spend the day out in nature.

Around 9:30a.m. that morning while leaving home all had the makings of a perfect day. All the neighborhood kids were away in school, the morning rush hour traffic had subsided as by now most commuters had reached their appointed destinations and then he began to explore the town armed with just his favorite cup.

This cup had sentimental meanings to him because his kids made it especially for his birthday. It was not a very well made cup, the handle was broken and it had a crack alone the base which cause it to slowly leak whenever it was used but he treasured this cup dearly and would use no other.

The beginning of the journey was reminiscent of old times before, Mrs. Johnson was getting an early start with her yard work and preparing for the fall colors. Mr. Bill was loading his truck in anticipation of picking up a fresh haul of vegetables that he often sold at the local market, and the Robinson's' set out the trash containers as today was collection day. Everyone knew and respected Bob for he had resided in the neighborhood for a very long time. It was a great day.

After a couple of hours of roaming around and enjoying the sites Bob noticed a new mall that had recently opened in his area. Always wanting to visit this large new grand establishment, he thought, why not now? It was lunch hour anyway so the timing could not have been more perfect.

Once inside Bob was truly amazed with all the grand and splendid beauty that was applied. There must have been at least one hundred department stores and specialty shops from all around the world.

Breath-taxingly, inside at the center of attention was this huge atrium featuring a water fall, a gazebo and a spacious food court/ meeting area. This space contain some twenty-seven eateries of assorted cuisine with the center of attention surrounding a live band performance.

The band performed excellent. They were familiar with most of the latest hits and popular tunes. Everyone loved them.

Bob order coffee and decided to stay and listen for a while.

When his coffee arrived he realized that this musical phenomenon had attracted a crowd so large that his view was obstructed so he decided to move closer to the front for a better view.

Before long his moment of pleasure was interrupted. He noticed the sound of a "pluck"; the type of a sound that is made as an object strikes water or in this case a liquid. The sound then repeated and became frequent before Bob looked up and noticed that the crowd of people began to gather around him and each taking turns dropping coins and paper bills into his newly purchased cup of coffee.

Completely caught off guard by this action Bob was speechless. He felt embarrassment, humiliation and totally belittled by this occurrence. Bob immediately left to return to the safety and comfort of his own home.

Still humbled by the effects of the actions earlier in the day he could not help but ask himself while on the way home, "Why me?", "Why did it have to be me?"

Just then as Bob was about to cross the street the traffic light changed to red requiring him to remain at the corner a little while more. While he waited on that corner with tears rolling down his cheeks from the embarrassment that he faced he noticed that the sound of the "pluck" had returned.

Once again people passing by who could see this gentle man with tears in his eyes and holding ever so tightly to this pitiful looking cup began depositing coins and paper currency into his cup.

Now the poor guy was devastated so he quickly hurried home to barricade himself behind closed doors and just sat there for a moment to try and gather his own thoughts. What could cause this kind of a reaction?, he wondered. " A perfectly good cup of coffee had been ruined!", he exclaimed. But even more disturbing to him than anything else was the fact that the value he placed on his special cup had been desecrated.

Eventually, Bob set aside his thoughts and began the task of cleaning up his precious cup and the mess that was made by the crowds. Upon tallying the sums of the collectibles he received for the day, Bob counted a total of $214.68.

Suddenly a smile came across his face as he started to chuckle hardy. Realizing now what had happen his laughter grew harder and harder. It grew so loud in fact, that Bob fell out of his wheelchair.

These days it's told around town that old Bob now visits the mall some two or three times a week. I understand that should you happen to visit that mall in his area then he shouldn't be to hard to spot. He'll be the guy sitting up near the front drinking coffee from his now bronzed cup.

And oh yeah, should you happen to see Bob, don't forget to leave him some change.

CHAPTER THREE
HONORABLE MENTIONS

In the beginning, while trying to cope with such a devastating blow with repercussions ranging from inconvenience to paralysis to death, the fall continued.

"What's that?", you say. " Now I'm confused!" The ground should've broken the fall and with all these caring people surrounding me to protect me from further harm, what else could go wrong?

Well, this could take a spell so pull up a seat and sit right down.

The first thing to go was my job then next the friends soon to be followed by the family, the house and eventually the wife.

I tell you these things that happened must have had some medicinal or therapeutic value because my neck didn't hurt nearly as much anymore.

Over a twenty year period after compiling a successful history in the field of building engineering with approximately fifteen of those years being served as "Chief Engineer", my legacy will include many of the great hotels that I have had the pleasure of working with. This list includes; Crowne Plaza, Holiday Inn's, Wyndahms and Radissons. It's true that the chances are pretty slim that you'll ever meet people like "Princess DI" at any of these locations, however, each facility carries in itself a world-wide reputation. Alone with this history came the trend of being known as the "measuring stick", wherein, if you wanted to know how good you were the answer was found by being compared to me.

For the most part my services had been rendered to different branches on several properties. There have been times of dubious distinction when my services have been rendered to competitors simultaneously. It was not unusual for the phone to ring with a job offer being on the other side of the receiver and if my resume' floated the electronic highway it was not to request an interview but simply to announce my intentions which almost always spelled sudden death to anyone who'd dare be the competition.

Employers once acquainted with me often marveled at the opportunities to restore alliances when and should the possibilities present themselves, which leads us to this story.

Upon restoring a relationship with a property that I had previously shared a three plus year prior history with our developments continued just like before. You know that magic moment when you see old friends whom you haven't seen in a while or that separation between you and that special someone when no ones to blame, well, once again we became the talk of the town.

It was not long before we were once back into that all too familiar position as leaders of the franchise and the title of the "go to guy" was strapped again around my waist where it so rightfully belonged.

Tragedy struck!!! After barely surviving a brush with death the immediate reaction and response, which I did, was to contact my employer and notify them of my pending situation. This injury caused me the lost of a successful campaign as Chief Engineer and the reward I received for remaining a consummate professional was termination. Reason being, "out of work for three days". This reward was granted to me on exactly the third day. How fortunate of a person I must be, I thought to myself, to have such loyalty, devotion and swift reactions bestowed on my behalf. I was flabbergasted not to say the least and kind of pissed, too. Accompanying this memorial event was the fact that insurance was non-existent, but who really needs insurance at times like these, right? Right!!!

There were no visits from co-workers; not even a get well card! It's a good thing that we were all friends. I shutter to think what would have happen had we been enemies, I probably would have received a cement necktie.

Some of my devoted following even had the audacity to call me at my bedside for solutions and directions on making repairs. Surely you've guessed by now that most of my suggestions began with "stick it up @#&?#............. At this point it's a fair assumption that this once so sweet relationship has now gone sour.

But don't cry for me Argentina! Granny always said, "every advantage has a disadvantage and each disadvantage has an advantage." For me advantages came in several forms; first, being was not having to return to the presence of such ingrates, but the more time that I spent pondering the event revealed to me in truth that my job situation was nothing more than a dead-end. The heights of my field had already been achieved years ago and any continued longevity or movement would have only served as lateral.

Opportunity was now available for me to explore new fields. Confinement to the "time clock" and the "powers to be" was removed. There was no more fighting traffic jams or no more missing the kids recitals at school because of work. No more power struggles or jockeying for position with some butt-kissing college grad who hadn't yet developed pubic hairs. I'm free I tell you, freeeeeee!!!

The word <u>retirement</u> suddenly has a very sweet appeal to it. Now with destiny back in my control and time as a instrument of leisure you may address me as Mr. Joe Q. Public. Sure, you know that guy who comes here all the time and will never leave more than a dollar tip. He always sits at your table and you can't wait until he leaves and hopes he never comes back. But he just keeps on coming and coming and coming. Well, in defense of Mr. Public, he has already paid his dues to society and this is life's comical way of re-cycling by making some one else pay. It don't get much better than this.

As time goes on the creativity and ingenuity has a way of resurfacing to the fore-front thus removing the boundaries of confinement. Had I not been injured I would have continued being a slave to reality in my mind and convincing myself of how fortunate I had been to still be working, ultimately, never knowing or experiencing the freedom or fulfillment that I now know. The freedom of while still at a very young age, to travel and vacation on demand. Then there's the luxury to began each day with the time and directions being of my own choosing and then there's the option to work if I want to and if I don't then that's okay, too.

You know, I even heard the birds sing one of natures overtures, a sound so loud and clear but yet soft and gentle that had been long forgotten because they would sometimes get lost with the sounds of car engines going by as everyone fights to try and find their place in the human rat race. Boy!, if only my friends could see me now.

FRIENDS - Webster's dictionary defines as an ally; supporter or sympathizer. That's just simply another case of strong words with no meaning. Never being one to consider myself with a lot of friends because of the weight such relationship would bear, I'd over a period of time formed a bond with two individuals whom I now realized were confused to be friends.

This first individual I met during a job interview upon a that property he was tasked on to revive from the ruins of mediocrity. It was not a wonderful job and the pay sucked, as a matter of fact it was below the average of what I was already making. This guy didn't attempt to window dress his situations. He spoke candid, honestly and about his intentions to succeed. Before long this simple interview became a several hour conversation and together we had started to lay out plans for setting up a base of operation and a scheduling timetable was already in the works before we realized two very important things. He had not yet made me a job offer and I had not yet accepted. A team was born.

The early days were so disastrous that upon arriving to work at 7 o'clock a.m., you could run from one major problem to the next non-stop sometimes until 7p.m. We liked to call it "putting out fires". The heart was racing, the adrenaline was flowing, it was a great challenge and I loved it. Pretty soon this property that was viewed as the big bad beast of burden had submitted to defeat. No stones were left unturned. What was once considered the laughing stock in the industry had now become the best kept secret in town. Ratings soared and mutual respect and admiration for each others professional skills and abilities soon spilled over into each others personal abilities and soon a bond was formed. Tensions began to ease up a bit and we finally started to trust each other.

My counterpart had been raced in Pittsburgh living in rural America, then moved to Denver, so coming to Atlanta for a place of settlement was an awakening experience. Its not the first nor the last case of culture shock known when people come to this city for the first time due to it's ethnic diversity.

My skills, ability and intelligence was not an issue from the beginning because there was a job that needed to be done, however, now that everything was under control I became perceived as a threat to his employment position. We had some battles. We had some wars. A couple of times there we almost came to blows, and then we found each others heart. We became friends. We became inseparable. Like Siamese twins joined at the hip, twin brothers with different moms, we were "buds".

Eventually the property could no longer sustain the continual growth of both our salaries so my counterpart exercised his options elsewhere that presented more challenges, more recognition,and most of all more money. This not only gave both of us room to grow financial it game me, the new commander-in-chief a vacancy to fill.

So here comes this fat head kid be-bopping into my office one day with all the tale-tell signs that his next appointment with MacDonald's for a couple of 'happy meals' was not far away. All the body language was wrong and it was obvious no one ever tried discussing etiquette with this guy.

His resume' was pretty much none existent, his job school related transcripts were impressive but upon further interview it became apparent that he had no idea of what he was doing. Just another waste of my time in an already busy day. Then he spoke of willingness to learn, the desire to be independent and wanting to do something positive with his life. In him I saw sincerity, character and the chance to make a difference in an already negative world, so I decided to give him a chance.

No one ever said it would be easy! I'd swear at times this kid must have had ten thumbs and two left feet. To say challenging would be an understatement, but aside from the detailed business of learning the job at hand we ventured into areas of management, image, public relations and personal goals and expectations. It became my personal ambition to give this young person every bit of knowledge, advantage or opportunity at my disposal. This kid became my unofficial adopted son. Then the cycle repeated itself. Where there was two soon became three. The three amigos.

So as the story goes we become the three amigos all resting snugly in charge of our own respective property. Seems sometimes though life has a way of dealing it's own cards when you least expect it. It's just the mark of the man on how you play the cards you're dealt. And as expected, misfortune began to rear it's ugly head with the first casualty being the gentleman from Pittsburgh. For one reason or another his new employers were not as impressed with him as he was with himself. As well as you can imagine this action of termination left the poor soul crushed, a mere shell of the man he used to be. He'd gained an unwanted reputation among the circuit as the man unable to get the job done.

In keeping with things that friends do for each other I communicated with him several times a week with inquiries of the pending job search while often sharing information regarding upcoming vacancies before they were made public notice. Well, just like good news travels fast so does bad reputations and this attachment seemed to have taken a pretty good hold. No one would hire him, not even the little old lady next door. Depression was no longer an option at this point since he had been out of work for some six months now with a new house payment and car payment due. These items were the remnants of celebrations from his new previously short lived job.

The only control at my disposal right now was an assistance position, a bit of a role reversal if you will. Wasn't long before I was able to make him realize that our relationship was more important than any stupid title could be and besides it's a fact that it's easier to find a job when you have one than it is when you don't. Alas, we were reunited again and it felt good. One more dragon to slay.

Clichés become such supposing based upon a bunch of truths which would explain why misery loves company. No sooner than one situation is laid to rest before another arises. Chief Engineers were being tossed around like salad. This time it was my newly acquired son. The sudden rise to power just as rapidly inflated an already as previously mention fathead and ultimately became his demise. Once again that upcoming car payment and school tuition comes into play. So in doing what friends do I secured a place for him on my staff without any lost in pay from his last job. Where there was two now there are three. The three amigos together once more.

Earlier the following year my services would be re-acquired by a former employer that would later turn out to be a nemesis; however, this move created room for growth and allowed Pittsburgh to advance from number two to number one and my adapted son would move from number three to number two. All were happy again. Although locations were again different we constantly remained in touch with each other and made time to hang out together. This was a five and four year relationship respectively and you just don't throw this kind of thing away, you know?

Well, half way into the year came the misfortune of my accident. The news got out as soon as possible to everyone whom it may have concerned.

It was a very emotional and trying time for me when fear of the unknowing was more demanding than the actual pain in itself.

My adapted son managed to steal away from his very busy schedule one visit to see me on which occasion he brought me a pack of cigarettes. Mr. Pittsburgh on the other hand faired much better, he visited three times and promised to come back but never did. Soon six months passed. *Et tu Brute'.*

Remember, D.T.A., and that stands for don't trust anybody.

You know, it's funny, somehow and for some reason the persons that I did not hold personally as high regards as friends came to see and visit me more often than the ones who were supposed to be.

Perhaps it was just to see if I was dead, and/ or maybe, just to verify that I was really bad off and to celebrate the victory, I don't know.

I never really understood or found an advantage in this action I must say unless it's just the fact that now you know who your friends are. That's really some small comfort, though. To continue to try and force this relationship from my standpoint seem futile because after all it was my turn to need an ally, supporter and sympathizer. So to you, Mr. Webster this is my footnote from personal experience, sir, delete that word from your vocabulary because there is no such thing as a **friend.**

Who needs friends anyway? That's what family is for, you know, "blood is thicker than mud", "they'll be there for you through thick and thin", "the last one to let you down". Yeah, you've heard 'em all before.

This brood of mine turn out to be an interesting one. The first out pour of visiting disbelievers, well wishers and rubber - neckers was simply astonishing. This first wave of gathering was so impressive until I found myself wishing it was someone else that was laying there with a broken neck just so I could participate. These kind of things generally only happens at funerals. My ex-lovers would come together and be kind to each other offering rides and consolidations and actually being civil. It was beautiful, I tell you, b-e-a-u-t-i-f-u-l. Like having an out of body experience. It has to be pretty similar, just lying there being unable to move but fully aware of everything going on around you while people talk at you or about you as though you no longer exist.

As people crowded into the room one by one the initial thoughts for concern might be that this injury might be far worst than I first imagined. Nah, what could possibly be worst than having a broken neck and never being able to utilize any of the limbs of your own body for the rest of your life.

Suddenly panic struck. The only remaining possibility left is that my conditions had worsened and turned fatal meaning I wouldn't be long left on this earth. That though offered in many ways a sigh of relief until I realized how selfish I was being and then began grieving about the undo additional hardship and burden this effect would have on my surviving family members.

As the secret whispers and private conversations constantly grew into a roar it became the focus of my attention, you see, it wasn't like I had anywhere to go or something to do before the primary purpose of all this attention soon came to light. What was most important right now to them was not the severity of my condition but simply how soon would I be able to return to work.

These two ladies although ex's were still deeply embedded into the linings of my pockets to the sums of $700.00 a month each for child supports and did not care to have their checks interrupted. This new found information made me feel much better.

By this time my concentration swiftly turned to thoughts of the occult, Miss Rudolph, mental telepathy or anything that would allow me the gift of moving heavy objects and levying them upside their heads. Something as simple as a cup of water in my hand combined with a well timed muscle spasm at this point would have been well received.

Don't you feel the love here this morning? Since we are such a loving group and me the man of the hour and just like before always in control of the most disastrous situations, I calmly reminded these two visions of loveliness about the pending insurance, social security and veterans administration claims.

The saying that music soothes the savaged beast was never more apparent. One might have thought I was playing a violin concerto in a den filled with lions as those viscous roars turned once again to smiles. Hair weave was floating in the air freely, everywhere, while they were dancing to the tune of "Money, Money, Money" as sung by the O'Jays. All was calm again.

Now surely you didn't believe that, did you?

Okay, so what when it comes to paperwork the government operates with the efficiency of dragging snails, but six months!!!, who'd have every though it? So the bickering continues. There was another word that is my personal preference but my kids may someday be reading this so for now I'll tender my thoughts.

After several months, multiple phone calls and tons of paper work later relief was not far from sight. I couldn't quite make out what it was but it was coming to me in the form of a man. Could it be a spirit?, there's stories that's been told about premonitions and occurrences of this sort. It could be the Lord, for it's been told how He comes to those who believe. It's getting closer and closer and starting to take form. I can see it clearly now and it's headed this way, it's the United States postmaster and he's carrying a check. And in the background you can hear the chorus refrain, "hallelujah."

Just when you though it would be safe to go back in the water; "low and behold", social security reduced each mother of their payments by $600.00 and under the V.A. guidelines neither was eligible for claims.

As for me, well, social security paid one/third of my previous salary with a matching third pending coming from the veterans administration. The $1400.00 a month for child support was no longer being deducted out of my pay and the extremely high payroll deductions came to a squeaking halt.

It's all so ironic now because my annual is still down by a third but I'm actually bringing home more money than ever before. For the first time in a long while my income tax will likely break even, even if there is no return.

Meanwhile, the disappointed mothers now call me the "mauther..." and will have very little to do with me since my role of Mr. Moneybags has diminished. My telephone rings so seldom now that no one is calling me in the need for money that sometimes I find myself picking up the receiver just to check the dial tone.

Finally the benefits of what has taken many years of toil and labor are beginning to ripen as I sit here sipping on an ice **cold** brew and looking out the window while I wait on the mailman.

It's been said that everything happens for a reason so if this is the reason then let it be. (An exert from Paul McCarthy).

Alas, all this relief did not come without further penalties. You've got to keep in mind now that I'm still falling and just because my head hit the floor that was only the beginning of the consequences of my fall. And also keep in mind that at this point I'm as helpless as a new born baby having to learn how to feed myself, how to write and even how to dress myself for the first time using foreign aides and equipment.

Since this new found wealth is ultimately some six months in the rear another of the problems it caused was debts with creditors. Some were willing to be tolerant and some were not. The one creditor I needed the most at this time was my house where I was raised and had been living and paying off the mortgage for several years since my return to the state.

First of all, a couple of bad decisions were made here, one being taking out a second mortgage on a property that had already been paid for and the second was doing business with family members.

During an era when my tenure was to travel the world life was good and prosperous on the home front. So good in fact that it induced greed into the hearts of men. This time it was my parents. Maybe it came out of boredom or something, I'll never know and it's never really been explained to my full understanding.

One day after living in a house for about thirty years that had been purchased and paid for that wicked flyer arrived in the mail stating “money to lend to home owners”. A temptation to strong for even the weakest man to refuse. Against the advise of educators, financiers and a few people who just knew it was a deal to good to be true they decided to go ahead and take a dive into the pool of high interest loans.

When the money arrived it was like Christmas in July with no definite intentions, goals or game plans in site. Maybe it was just the thrill of having a large sum of money in hand at one time. Cars were purchased, clothes were bought and jubilation spread all around. Once the appetites of squandering had been fulfilled now it was time to come up with a plan.

So today we’ll remodel the house and remodel the house we did. After making several extensive repairs and several unnecessary additions the course of direction now shifted. Today we shall buy another house and buy another house we did. One problem though, instead of having a high interest loan to repay off now there were two high interest loans to repay off. The obvious solution seemed to be not far from hand simply rent out the old house and use the money to make the payments. Great idea only one more problem, though, no takers.

Over a period of time having to make two mortgages each month was starting to take a considerable financial toll coupled with the fact that the economy at this time was not at it’s best and work began drying up across the land. Realization sat in that this may have been a bad decision, but of course now it was a bit too late to be second guessed.

Well, who’s better to bail there parents out of a bad situation than their one and only son and that’s where I come in. Johnny on the spot. First it didn’t seem like such a bad idea. I was already familiar with the neighborhood since after all it was home, therefore, it made relocating quiet a cinch. Then time pasted. Resources at the big house began to dry up further and then there came to play a couple of health related issues. But of course, my role increased, not only do I save the farm but also I became a silent financial supporter. This was exactly what I needed, another cross to bear. Never-the-less, it was too late to turn back now.

During my injury months went by faster than a June bug in July and with each passing month came one more reminder that another bill was due. At this point I began to wonder if it would ever end. The moneys that arrived seemed to have been the equivalent of too little too late. The mortgage could have been saved but at this time there were no additional incomes at the big house and my inability to be the silent provider over this period of time made me the odd man out. That's right I lost and remember I'm cripple. But still there's more to come.

So heading into late November the Christmas tree goes up in preparation for the holidays when the shocking news arrives that the house was up for sale and should close on about the 3rd of January. In defiance of being denied a celebration packing began with the tree remaining in tact through out the whole ordeal.

Have you ever tried house or apartment shopping on a fixed income? Please believe me it's virtually impossible. There was not enough money to qualify anywhere and my benefits were too much to receive assistance. That's right, now I'm homeless and cripple at Christmas time. Merry Christmas to you, too.

I found myself in a situation whereas I was being told to get out when I couldn't even get up.

With time rapidly approaching there's was no other alternative but to sallow some pride and humble myself and become a live in of a care taker. We'll be back to this subject in a later chapter.

By now you're probably trying to figure out what good came from this scenario. There was the fact that no matter what the odds or the obstacles I could survive but not only just survive, but to do it with some sense of dignity. There was the fact that the house at this time needed further repairs and adaptations to be wheelchair compliance to the sum of some $25,000.00. And there was the fact that the work was to have begun approximately two weeks after the decision to sale was made.

It served as an awakening of the first law of the land, "self preservationist first." And more over, don't do business with family, 'cause remember they'll be the last ones to put you down.

Okay, so it comes to this, me and my wife, you and me against the world until death do us 'part. Fortunately it didn't quiet have to come to that but there were some tense moments for a while.

Of course we functioned like most normal married couples in middle-aged America. We both worked and she spent the money, soon only I worked and she spent the money and finally nobody was working and she was still spending the money.

Came a time there when I really could have kicked some tail but my feet wouldn't move so we end up talking about it. When the talking was over she'd go out and spend the money.

We had a wonderful relationship and great communications. Besides she was a very frugal shopper and bought only the things that we absolutely had to have. Take for instance that swamp land in Florida, we needed that for ah.., ah.., ah.., well, surely that Brooklyn bridge purchase had to be a good idea 'cause why would you want to go all the way to Brooklyn and can't get across.

We had the best of everything, magazine subscriptions to over forty-seven publications, members of the book of the month club and all the fine valuable goods received from the likes of "Finger Hut" and the "Home Shopping Network". Why, we had it all.

Ours was a very good working relationship, when she worked. I left home at 5 o'clock in the morning and returned at 6 p.m. and my wife left home at 3:30p.m. and returned at 2a.m. Had not it been for this foolish injury we'd have made twenty years standing on our heads.

Once I became injured this Florence Nightingale was constantly by my side. For a while there it took a considerable amount of effort to distinguish the visitor from the patient. Even the hospital staff often got us confused. Personally and later on it was revealed the factor of being in the house alone and the fear of now being the one in charge of taking care of responsibilities came into play.

Sure, there were a lot of financial responsibilities on my part with never enough money to go around but my part was that of a financial aggressor. Only debts with the utmost importance got immediate attention everyone else got "forget it". And the threats of bad credit risk came as a joke, heck, I was already in debt up to my neck that couldn't be paid so why would I have a need for any more.

Like a symphony conductor I'd direct and orchestrate directions and compositions from my death bed because it was unbearable to think of the pain and loneliness this angel would have to face all alone. The directions that I left to follow were so clear, even a child could understand. Perhaps, I should have given them to a child.

Well, the credit card payments went to the gas company, the gas payment went to the water utilities and so on and so on. Now I'm up a creek without a paddle. Accompanying this fine mess is additional late charges, restoration fees and accrued penalties and interest.

Today my departure from the hospital came without a hitch signaling the end to a great vacation. It has been such a long time since care free days and personal service was at my disposal. By any means it'll be great to be back home again or so I thought. To my wondering surprise all had the picturesque quality of normality and surprised I was to learn that it was that, just a picture.

Forced into a situation of having to leave the comfort of my bed in order to try and salvage the household survival, troubles erupted. When knowledge of the day to day activities became aware to me I became the problem. Expectations of me in my present condition was to stay shut up in a room all day and be at the mercy of my keeper while she and my stepdaughter were out spending the money. They were having the time of their life before I ruined it all by getting discharged from the hospital. In retaliation for this knowledge medications and foods were deliberately withheld or delayed from me automatically aggravating an already volatile situation. Thus, in return for little or no support I cut off all financial support. Now it was full scale war.

War prevailed for a while and reconciliation even became an option but was quickly ruled out. With a friend like this who needs enemies?

Some good did come from this ordeal, at least I no longer had to eat her meals. Secondly, the anger helped fuel the determination for recovery so as soon as I was able to raise my leg high enough to reach her butt I politely kicked her to the curb.

Thankfully I found myself at the end of my fall, reaching a final resting place where I could catch my breath and try to began to get back up again. Stripped butt naked now that there was nothing else left to loose and no more to give. It should have probably been a depressing time but for me it served as a time for cleansing.

Afforded perhaps the most greatest and valuable opportunity life has to offer is the chance to start a new life without any leftover baggage. A chance to pick and choose a course of direction this time knowing the consequences that it may bring.

Somewhere it's been written that "all that don't kill you will make you stronger", well, I didn't die, I just got stronger. The skin is thicker now and the mind much more tougher. Compassion has been thrown out the window and for this made me a better person by being true to myself first.

With this rare opportunity came the chance to look death in the eye and see the peace and calm after the storm. To have an out of body experience and in essence see my own funeral and the disgust and lack of concern displayed on my behalf once I was no longer worthy of making financial contributions. And to you all goes my thanks for giving me the chance to find your true value while there is still time to do something about it. It also seemed to have given everyone else a reality check as to just how difficult life is without me.

So this is to serve as public notice to everyone whom it may concern, when the event of my death does arrive, don't come to my funeral with fake tears in your eyes trying to see what I left behind. There won't be any wills or insurance policies to fight over, everything I have left will be canceled or liquidated before I go.

As a matter of a fact, this reminds me of a little poem I read sometimes back and when my time has come I want this to be used as my eulogy:

When I'm in a sober mood.
I worry. work and think,
And when I'm in a drunken mood
I gamble, play and drink.

But when my moods are over
And my life has come to pass,
I hope they bury me upside down
So the world may kiss my a__!.

CHAPTER FOUR
ROLE MODEL

As much as things may change some things remain the same. In my portfolio there will exist no denial of me being an arrogant, egotistical and stubborn son-of-a-gun. There will be a number of reference of exchanges in reference to the always aggressive and competitive style I display. Remaining in tact where ever my talents have been released will be in effect written documents and physical monuments to continually serve as a guideline and a testament to the leadership ability that I demanded and portrayed.

To lead by example and be willing to go head first into battle has always been an admirable qualification at my disposal. To be willing to accept and carry out these responsibilities with sometimes the lost of personal sacrifice but never compromising the lost of dignity, the lack of character or the void of pride is what makes this role so special and rare. The mere knowledge of having others come to you for guidance and leadership with the distinction to possibly influence there lives forever.

This is in by no way a responsibility to be taken lightly.

With great honor and pleasure, I take this time to take my hat off to my kids whom I love and cherish so much. ***Joab, Eddie, Chanel, Ernestine, and last but not least Nickolas.*** You guys are the only constant in my life and the source of my motivation. The pride and joy you guys bring is so magnificent that I want the whole wide world to know.

Often we have sometimes have had to endure some difficult struggles and we've survived. Sometimes things don't always go our way but we keep our heads held up high. And though some things might come by pretty hard we never stop trying, and I love you all.

I want to thank you for the strength, character and style you display and posses. Although you gave me smiles, hugs and kisses when I was laid up in the hospital I could see in the back of your eyes the tears, the pain and the suffering you must have carried in those tiny little hearts. I want to thank you for being there because without the sound of your voices and the music you make when you laugh, without that tough guy character you try to display when you are concerned; without you, I don't know if I'd have had enough strength or motivation to carry on.

This will no doubt be the most difficult challenge that we have ever had to face before. The battle will indeed be a long and tedious one. The progress will definite be slow and at times it'll seems that there is no end in sight. You all have had the good fortune of being blessed with the opportunity to take in first hand knowledge of a living testament on how the most debilitating of obstacles can be overcome.

It gives me great pleasure to have the chance to share this lesson with you. I know I will survive this journey and you all will come away with more valuable resources than you could ever know.

From this example you shall witness commitment, determination, character, love and devotion, courage and the grace in which this victory will be achieved. This shall serve as a demonstration for how all the things you have learned over the years should come together. This is vintage BURLEY and this obstacle only presents itself as another opportunity for me to be a role model.

CHAPTER FIVE
IT'S ACCEPTABLE

Hi there; let's take a few minutes to cover an area of something I'd like to refer to as "FYI" or For Your Inf. This section is intended to cover some areas and subject matters that may be of a personal issue, vulgar in stature or may have the appearance of seeming somewhat offensive in nature. However, please be advised that the views and opinions discussed in this chapter do solely and directly reflect those of the writer.

Opening day, the beginning of baseball season, forget that grapefruit league stuff. The beginning of spring, weathers good, the whole nine yards. Then, to make matters better, you're fortunate enough to be living in Atlanta. Home of the Braves, America's team. Undeniable the best team in baseball for the past ten years. And who really cares what you think this is my book.

Anyway, the stadium constantly sells out, I mean who wouldn't thrive at the opportunity to become a part of history each time these guys play. The team knows that too. In the interim, to try best they can to compensate everyone without denying themselves the opportunity to remain the money hoarding sharks that they are, they present this public relations packet called "standing room only" tickets for the mere asking price of one US dollar bill.

What a bargain you might say. Well, here's where I come in.

For the same dollar fare all I have to do is plop myself down into my wheelchair and move up front to the rail. One of the best views in the stadium and at options can take my kid with me. If it's an older kid they can push you or if it's a younger kid then they can ride in your lap. I mean who's going to complain! Talk about getting your money's worth; where else can you get first class family entertainment for only a buck?

Go, BRAVES!!!

* * *

Let's say it's Wednesday or Thursday, whatever, but you know that day when your annoying aunt or mother-in-law comes by. It could even be that prayer group from the church featuring sister Betty, with her self righteous ways who just so happens to be sleeping with Deacon Robinson. So the names might have been changed to protect the innocent but you all know who you are and besides we all have one.

You really don't care to be bothered by those folk irregardless of their reasons or why. Searching your mind and heart for reasons they would leave early or simply not come you come up blank. That old I'm sleepy routine or the excuse about not feeling well just don't seem to work as well anymore.

So try this on for size. You like ice cream, don't you? Then pick your favorite flavor, cuddle right up in front of the television with a nice movie or video, and eat until you heart is content. Don't worry about the calories, that's not the reason we are here. Besides, we'll cover that area later.

Even if you are calorie conscious, you will still have to eat so try milk, taco's, beans, onions, etc.. Anyway, I think by now you should know where I'm going with this. If you hadn't figured it out yet then I'll break it down for you slow folk.

All right, here comes the party of five, with their self righteous, indigenous ways and you want them to go. Also, by now that old belly of yours should begin to bloat as you start to swell inside from the gas encountered from he remnants of the diet before.

Just let it rip. That's right, let it rip. Brrrpp! Don't be ashamed, just let it go. If they try to ignore it or pretend it didn't happen then do it again to solidify your point. Brrrpp! Blow it out your rear!

You'll be surprised at how all of a sudden everyone remembers something else they have to do, or somewhere else they need to be. Nobody's really going to be critical about your actions because they'll be willing to attribute it to your condition. Whatever the reason the results are the same. You got rid of them.

* * *

You went to the cupboards to get a snack and your favorite food is all gone. The game is on the tube or there's friends over, you go to the 'frig just to find out that you're out of brew. Not a problem. Hop into the vehicle, down to the market and do what you've got to do.

Keep in mind, this is not a not for profit situation. Everybody's trying to get paid.

If your position is ambulatory, such as, you're on crutches, walkers or other prosthesis equipment designed to aide in your mobility then press one now.

"One"— be especially mindful of carpets, rugs, uneven floors and anything that might constitute a tripping hazard.

My personal favorites; visit the fruit and vegetable department. Grapes, even though so every delicious also make for excellent slipping devices once coupled with prior disabilities or the sympathy of the compassionate few spells: Ching, ching!!! Money in the bank.

The dairy department is another good reliable candidate. For some reason there almost always seems to be a spill in the dairy department, be it milk, juice, cheese, you name it. Probably cause kids like to run through there and try to be helpful. Thanks guys.

But the easiest, which is more like a free coupon or something is the infamous "WET FLOOR" sign. May as well just lay the money on the table and walk away. True enough there's always going to be spills of some sort that needs to be cleaned up but most stores have the tendency to clean up during peak hours or high traffic areas. Don't inconvenience yourself for their blunders.

Surely, you've had several courses or classes on how to fall without being re-injured irregardless to what center you recuperated from. Hon these skills and use them to your fullest advantage.

Should in the event you become one of the fortunate few to find yourself in this position, just remember to lay there until Ken Nugent gets you a check cause he'll get you the money and he'll get it fast. Just watch the commercials on television.

* * *

You may find this pretty interesting, too. You've been out to lunch at some eatery, a kind of sit down and eat restaurant, nothing fancy and you've enjoyed your meal and you're ready to leave. Here you may head to the cashier. Upon approaching you notice that the line is quite long. After standing there for a few minutes you began to tire.

"Scene-one" — Leave your position, walk straight up front and jump ahead of the line. Nobody's going to really mind and even if they do then they won't say anything for fear of being ridiculed by the crowd.

"Scene-two" — Leave your position and go sit out front in the waiting area. Everyone will understand and many will offer some condolences for your situation. This you simply can not refuse.

Endless possibilities exist here. First, this could mean you will never have to wait in line again which in itself is a pretty good asset to have around. Especially when out shopping are trying to get sales. Second, you could sit in the waiting area for a few minutes and then get up and walk out the door without paying which could mean free lunch. Not bad, huh?

Should by chance you be one of those persons with a healthy appetite this little stunt could prove to be more beneficial than first expected. If you've got a date or a partner don't despair, it's quiet understandable if someone is there to open the doors or offer assistance to you.

Go ahead and do the math figuring this escapade at least a couple times a week times a year could really turn out profitable. It may even produce enough revenue to purchase those gold rims you've always wanted to go on your chair.

Don't forget to maintain a large selection of restaurants as to avoid frequently visiting the same one too often and becoming conspicuous.

If the though occurs to you of getting busted and possible arrested then consider this; this set of circumstances is pretty unusual and no one is prepared to deal with it so it makes it easier all around to try and make arrangements to work out a solution. Besides, police departments are not equipped to facilitate are even administrate the difficult and specific requirements you present. I mean what are they going to do, handcuff you to your chair? This problem of administering necessary drugs on a routine basis and administering bowel programs presence's a little more than a challenge.

By taking away your prosthesis equipment such as braces, crutches, chairs, etcetera...your mobility has been compromised thus requiring man power assistance throughout booking procedures. You have now become a pain in the butt.

It thus becomes feasible to have you detained at a medical facility where you can be better maintained or restricted to house arrest. Either way its still a pretty good deal plus you now receive more free meals.

And just think, this whole thing started out with a ten dollar lunch. Almost like a cheap vacation.

* * *

Here's one that seems to have become the most popular and is sure to be a crowd pleasure, Christmas time. "Joy to the world", "bah,...humbug!" That dreaded time of the year when you suddenly become everyone's favorite relative in exchange for that incredibly expensive present they've always wanted.

Well, just take that Christmas list and crumble it up into a little ball, then use it to practice your free throw shots in hopes of one day making it in the NBA. Forget the hassles of fighting traffic jams and the miserable elements from the seasons weather. Say good-bye to fighting crowds for the last of an item that's on sale. You know it's over priced anyway.

Instead stay in the comfort of your warm home, have another eggnog and finish watching your special program on television. You're not really expected to buy gifts since your means of incomes have become restricted, so why bother. Only the self-centered money grabbers would be indecent enough to ask you for anything in the first place. And you can best believe you didn't make their list.

But just in case you turn out to be one of those die-hard joy and love people then don't forget to take your handicap parking pass. Man!, those things are great. Irregardless, to where you are or how large the crowd is there are virtually always handicapped parking spaces available.

Just whip right in and park. No wasting time and getting frustrated looking for that illusive vacant space. Usually always located within just a few feet from the entrance, you can't beat it. Not to mention the self gratification of knowing that this space has been reserved specifically just for you.

Now, if you want to hustle a few dollars and help spread around that holiday cheer you can rent out your services for hire. Ride to the malls or the stores with a few desperate shoppers, hang your permit in the window and make money at the same time. Everyone will be grateful and you'll have money galore as your popularity increases when word gets around.

By the way, while you're out at these malls during the holiday seasons don't forget to bring alone your coffee cup and sit out in front of the stores for a while. This alone should increase your holiday budget by about twenty-five percent. Might as well take advantage of the holiday spirit while you're waiting on your shoppers.

However, don't be foolish enough to use your extra income on foolish Christmas gifts, instead use it to pad your bank account for those rainy days.

* * *

If ever you have experienced any of these situations or something somewhat similar, please feel free to share your stories with us. Inquisitive minds would like to know. Should you decide to try an experience for the first time then forward your results so that we might all share and learn from the outcome.

Stand by for the next episode of "IT'S ACCEPTABLE" to continue in a later chapter. Your views and opinions are welcomed.

You may feel free to contact us anytime at 1-800-DIS-ABLE.

(TO BE CONT'D.)

CHAPTER SIX
GETTING AROUND

When I woke this morning and looked down at my feet there was a sense of awe as I experienced a feeling of betrayal or the lost of something close and dear to me but in reality nothing could have been further from the truth. I soon discovered that under my control was one of the greatest commodities known to man at my disposal. Let's examine this.

How many times have you not felt well and needed to see the doctor, had an appointment or just plain not felt like getting out of bed today? I know that it's happened to me a time or two. Well, no problem, just lay back and relax, and take the bed with you. So go ahead and enjoy that second or third cup of coffee or you may just wish to finish seeing Judge Judy on TV. As your scheduled time grows near simply press in the call button on the side of you bed and an escort will soon arrive to take you where you need to be. Should in the event you fall back to sleep now that you are comfortably stretched out with several soft cushiony pillows and the warmth of layers of blankets around you someone will automatically search you out and see you to your appointed destination. If your travels should by chance have to consume a considerable amount of distance then that'll be arranged for you by your local travel agent or ambulance driver.

For instance today we decided to go on a field trip and we each had a lot of errands to run, maybe, a trip to the school, then the grocers, and perhaps a few hours at the mall. And for you women, that could translate to a few days at the mall. Well, as we all know this could require lots of back and forth traveling and has the makings of being a very long and exhausting day. Check this out, by just hopping into my chair traveling distances became less of a chore and required far less energy than I'd usually expend. I can just zip in and out of places with a breeze. Everyone else came back complaining of exhaustion.

Some models even come with battery power packs which makes travel even more comfortable and also comes in a wide assorted range of colors and styles. With new handy and easy to install accessory kits it is easy to carry a large quantity of items thus eliminating the necessity to make numerous trips back and forth. Best of all, the quality I seem to enjoy most is no more tired and achy feet.

Let's try another one. Let's say you're walking and after a lengthy journey your poor feet begin to feel like lead. "Boy, it sure would be nice if you didn't have to carry all this weight around", you think to yourself. Just as you succumb to the point of total exhaustion this person passes you by with a steady stride and no immediate signs of weakness or slowing down in sight. Suddenly, just as fast as he appeared he disappears and all that's left is a blur and a faint memory of what just happened. So while you are sitting here on the ground smoking a cigarette and trying to catch your breath back it comes to you, that person who just blew you off the road with the aide of crutches has the advantage because he can distribute his total body weight over a four point area as opposed to just two. And with that new lightweight aluminum material they're made of those things just slice through the wind with little or no resistance at all.

This one happens more than you would think and is much more pleasurable when it's a pretty girl involved. And the pretty girl thing has a better chance of happening when you leave your wife at home. Often I find myself taking these walks just to see what I can catch for the day. But let's get back to the story. So you're out walking getting some exercise or just enjoying nature and then this car, truck, van, whatever, pulls up beside you, rolls down the window and then asks the ultimate question; "Can I give you a lift somewhere?" Of course, you can, only a fool would say no. By the way, just drop me off at Daytona Beach.

But wait, there's more. Okay, let's say you're doing public transportation, you know, the bus or train. Well, I don't know about you but usually when it arrives in my area it's generally very crowded with little or no place left to sit. Well, that used to be the case but not anymore. So what it's crowded?, with priority seating in place I'm virtually guaranteed a seat each and every time upon entering this type of a facility. If you were on a job that offered free lunch as a benefit surely you would take advantage of it such as I intend to take full advantage of every opportunity afforded to me. If no one voluntarily gives up a seat then simply call for the conductor to rectify the problem. That's a sure way to get some buns moving.

Now, unless you live in some really isolated, remote area, like Cleveland, Ohio, (just kidding), then most metropolitan cities offer the service of a "L" van. This particular vehicle is equipped with a power lift ramp for those chair bound travelers and offers the assistance of a full time duty driver. This equipment is usually limited assess of six to twelve riders at one time which means no overcrowding. Of course, you'll need to apply early and probably have to meet some stipulations to qualify but you'll find that it is well worth the effort. A few things that are noteworthy; you'll receive a picture identification card upon approval, you then become eligible to purchaser fares for one\half the original price of admissions and last but not least, you may apply for a primary care assistant status which will allow one person to travel alone with you at no additional cost. But now get this, you must call ahead of time to pre-schedule your intent to travel and this is to include your departure and arrival times, one way or round trip, then you just sit back and wait. You'll receive a phone call to confirm your travel arrangements or to notify you that your car is on the way and these people will provide you with door to door service. That's right, pick you up at your home and deliver you to your destination through out the journey. Just think of it as your very own private, chauffeur driven limousine. You'll even have the opportunity to meet new people, catch up on the morning news or finish enjoying this lovely book.

You may also find it interesting to know that major transportation carriers such as Greyhound and Trailways Bus Lines offer similar discounted or half price fares as long as you purchase your tickets in advance, of course, that's provided you can stand to ride that long. But it works fine for me because I can spend more time with my kids who are only a hour away whether it's by bus or by car and the price by bus comes to only nineteen dollars round-trip. That's hardly anything to turn your nose up at.

I really don't have any information for you as far as the air lines are concerned because I haven't tried them yet, but I feel pretty certain that they, too, would be willing to accommodate.

Just keep in mind that it could prove to be political as well as financial suicide for any company or business not to be willing to be tolerant.

No brag, just facts.

CHAPTER SEVEN
TOUCHED BY AN ANGEL

"I met a little girl; sho' was fine,
pretty little thing, just about blew my mind."
"She took me home and made love to me;
I knew right then and there this is where I wanted to be."

The words of a song as sung by the immortal **MARVIN GAYE** repeatedly played over and over in my head as she entered the room; a vision so beautiful I knew heaven must have been missing an angel. When I saw her I froze, just like a deer caught up in a cars headlight; it seemed as if time had stopped and all stood still as her voice was the only sound I heard when she spoke. Literally, I had to pinch myself just to make sure that it was not a dream and I was asleep.

I sat there in awe dazzled with amazement like a silly schoolboy while searching for words to say, feeling to myself if death has come for me then please let it be now.

When she spoke her name the words arrived to me like a soft whisper in the night with all the delicate music of a songbird in flight. She had the gift of illumination for with each smile the entire room seemed to have brightened. As she moved about the room her hair of blonde and brown danced through the air with the gracefulness of a Monarch butterfly. This woman possessed all the beauty of a mid-April flowery spring day.

Nothing else really mattered to me any more except for the fact that I knew that I had to meet this girl.

I knew just how to approach her and exactly what I wanted to say when a sudden cold brush of reality slapped me in the face. How could I say anything to her or ever expect to stand a chance of making a place for me in her heart? …for while I sat there, I sat in a wheelchair. Here stood the chance for me to endure possibly the best thing that has ever happened to me in my life and now this opportunity was about to pass me by.

Oh, shattered dreams. The crudeness of life, with someone this lovely by my side guys would envy me from miles around. But I suppose it was just not to be, it seemed only just a dream. Nothing more could be expected at this point but compassion, sympathy, or a friendship. Fate had dealt me such a cruel blow.

Finally, while wiping back a tear as it fell from my eye I gathered enough strength to go over and speak. We talked of backgrounds; we talked of flowers; we talked of expectations and we talked of love. We talked for hours and it was like we had known each other forever. No way you could have convinced me this relationship was not meant to be. We have so much in common; we've shared the same joy's and pains, we were meant to be.

In light of all the darkness that was now going on in my life the heavens had finally opened up and shined it's rays of light down on me.

We talked so long in fact, that others had to come and interrupt our conversation in order to take care of the business at hand for it was her time for therapy; see, she was in a wheelchair, too.

Before she left she touched my hand and I will never be the same ever again.

I watched her as she went away thinking how unkind it was that something as wonderful as this moment had to come to an end. As she went away so left a little piece of my heart but that empty feeling was soon overcome with the elation's and anticipation's of being able to see her again.

We managed to have a brief encounter at the end of the day (but as far as I was concerned the rest of my life would not have been long enough), to exchange phone numbers, make arrangements for our next meetings but mainly it seemed just to confirm that what had taken place earlier in the day was real and not a dream.

It was real and I could not get home fast enough to continue the strings of conversations. We have fun. She tells me that I am silly and that I make her laugh but believe you me, if you could see this woman when she smiles you would love to make her laugh just as much as I do.

Conversations must have gone on sometimes unending and one might think that eventually there'd be nothing else left to talk about. But that never happened because every second of time that I spent with her was well worth talking about. When our spaces combined the entire outside world was excluded and nothing more existed but us two.

Every time available we'd meet. Brief encounters were taken advantage of at the slightest drop of a hat. We passed messages to each other in the halls, through family members and even through the staff. Yeah!, we became an item, and it never felt so good. We were good for each other.

It was like, when you're apart you can feel each others thoughts and seem to know what they are going through at any particular time. It's like, when you're alone in thought you can still smell the sweet fragrance of her perfume. It's like, when you're asleep at night you dream about her and you hurriedly wish away the night hours to give in to day-light just so you can she her again.

Each passing day our relationship grew closer and we went about our ways as carefree as a bird, ignoring all surroundings and relationships to time. When therapy was over I'd often visit her in her room. Sometimes from home transportation could be arranged to come back and visit with her in the afternoon hours.

Our families were cool. Whenever we could arrange time together they would go away and leave us alone. This feeling was so contagious it could not be concealed. Even strangers could pass by and feel the magnetic attractions of these two bodies.

I'll never forget the first time she kissed me. As I leaned over to feel the touch from her lips the world went into a slow motion orbit and the distance between us seemed larger than a football field. Anticipation nearly drove me wild trying to pair up my imaginations with my expectations. Closer and closer we'd get and still it'd seem, oh, so very far away. My heart is pounding faster and I'm about to pass out from a nervous exhaustion. Wouldn't that be something?, after all this long wait I'd pass out and still wouldn't know how it felt to be kissed by an angel.

We were finally there. The big moment arrived when her lips touched mine and if I hadn't died before then surely this time I succeeded. After what appeared to be a lifetime though in reality was just a few seconds, I opened my eyes and she was still there. Amazingly she knocked me off my feet, every time I kissed her I got weak.

My blood pressure was racing so fast until a passing cop threatened to give me a ticket for speeding.

If it was up to me this moment would have never end. But unfortunately, everything must end while we were disturbed by the un-expected sounds of our returning relatives. "Go away", I heralded my unanswered pleas to no avail, for nothing I could say would deter the fact that still it was time to go.

Is there no justice in this life? How can you give something and then take it away? Wouldn't it be better never to have known rather than to have loved and lost? I was a complete mess at this point, all I could do was to stand there in the middle of the floor pouting around like a spoiled little brat. Soon I admitted defeat and agreed that the day must come to an end.

We at this point had reached a whole new level as things began to accelerate. Everything started to move faster now, the feelings, the emotions, and the time. We had become so involved with each other that we somehow ignored that one destructive element that nothing has ever been able to survive:... *"time."*

The dark clouds of sadness rolled in while the thunderous sounds of reality struck it's deafening blows. Soon it would be time for her to return home hundreds of miles away and all the happiness found would soon be gone.

One more time life had it's turn to prove just how unjust it could be.

The remaining few days passed with the quickness of a winter breeze. Even the sun seemed to have dimmed. The falling leaves from the trees only seemed to have echoed the crying in my heart as though nature itself could understand the feelings we were going through.

It was so hard to see each other and try to talk when each time you meet you know that you've come one day closer to the time you won't be able to see each other again. We made the best of it but there is absolutely no way you can fill in the emptiness when there is a void in your heart.

Each time I looked into her eyes the tears of sorry would form. It was virtually impossible to conceal the way I felt. When we held hands, ah, it's so hard to explain, but you just never wanted to let go.

For those of you with kids, it's like when your baby goes to school for the first time. Deep inside your heart you know that it's a good thing for them but the selfish love you posses does not want to let them go. You're mixed with emotions because some of your tears are for joy and some are for sorry.

Unfortunately, the time had arrived. I could not sleep the night before because once it was daybreak again it would be the signal that it was time for her to go. But then I did go to sleep because it was the only way I could be alone with my girl in my thoughts. Besides, silly me, foolishly kept hoping that if I slept and did not wake then somehow I could prevent morning from coming and she would not have to leave.

We stayed together and held on to each other until the final piece of luggage was loaded onto the van. Now it was her time to go. This walk down the once warm and welcomed feeling hallway now felt so cold, desolated and lonely. This felt like a walk to a death sentence.

While she was being loaded into the van I held onto her hand until the last possible second. Then the door closed. Although I tried to remain strong my heart hit the ground with such a force that it would have registered a nine on the Richter scale.

Standing there waving good-bye while the van pulled away it was hard to see clear anymore as by now my eyes were misty when they filled with the tears that flowed. I just stood there for a while. And when the van was no longer in sight, I just stood there.

Eventually my sister came and laid her hand on my shoulder as to consoled me and make me face the fact that it was over. With my head hanging down and my heart broken we walked back to the car and headed for home. I was completely in a different zone, my world had come to an end.

The ride home was miserable. By the time my girl arrived home and settled in I could not wait to give her a call to make sure she was fine and to let her know how much I loved and missed her.

We constantly maintain contact on a regular basis. We exchange letters, cards and phone calls. We plan for the day that we can be together again, and I hope to be visiting her real soon.

What this lady has done to my life is phenomenal and can not be replaced. I owe her a lot of credit for being inspirational to me. I'm a very fortunate guy for having this ray of sunshine come my way. I've been blessed to have you in my world and I could not have met you if I had not been here.

This story should help serve as an awakening that love and relationships do not have to end because of a disability. As a matter of a fact it intensifies without the deception and betrayal that would be displayed otherwise.

My heart goes out to my angel who gives me a love and a friendship all so true. I hope out there somewhere that you can find an angel, too.

CHAPTER EIGHT
WORKING TOGETHER

Although it is important to have a strong support group in place at all times it becomes essential when one is in the process of trying to recover from a life changing event such as finding yourself physically challenged. Not only is it important to know that you are not alone in times like these but it becomes also important to learn the functions of these groups and how to take full advantages of the services they offer. It can increase your marketability, your exposure and your opportunities to succeed.

As a minority member it is possible to receive support through local and national chartered organizations, churches and some federally funded programs. Notification of your specific case requirements to local churches, radio and television stations have the potential of receiving air time which could result into donations and aide from the surrounding communities. This is in no way charity. These people simply understand the degree of difficulty involved in the struggle to survive when a person is with challenges and also have the presence of mind to understand that this problem is not limited to and could happen to anyone.

These people probably already have friends or family members who have experienced or suffered lost in similar situations. And more often than not, in our communities, issues such as insurance and major health care expenses are pretty much non-existent which often leaves permanently scared victims, broken homes and even to the possibilities of death due to the high cost of prescriptions.

As far as veterans are concerned, this is without a doubt the best prepared and organized avenue to pursue. This organization in itself is in no way removed from the line of needing improvement but in this area is probably to be considered the leaders of the pact.

Unfortunately, though, every disabled person is not a veteran.

As a veteran myself, I receive constant reminders and updates in the mail and through other venues, of the work, the privileges and other avenues afforded to me through the P.V.A. society, that stands for Paralyzed Veterans of America.

This veterans group has a well established network system already in place and tested that deals with situations such as small business, employment, education, recovery and so on. There are numerous cases on file where disabled veterans, although, not necessarily injured in the line of duty or while being on active service still received the support of this benefit.

Therefore, it should be fair and reasonable to extend this service to include all challenged people, that while not each and every challenged person had the distinct privilege or pleasure of serving their country by being on the front line, they were able to help serve by being loyal to the flag, supportive of our efforts and by paying taxes into this cause.

Well, after experiencing my time served as a physically impaired person I came to learn that many of the asistive devices designed as aides did not well serve their purpose simply for the fact that they were designed by people who had no clue of what it was like to be disabled. With this knowledge, specifically in my case with an engineering background, I was able to adjust, design and or create tools or devices that would better serve me and people with similar situations purposes.

This first hand knowledge led me to seeking out several patents which not only has the potential to be financial rewarding but most important of all will prove to be most beneficial by best aiding the very same people that it was designed to help.

The ground work for success is already prepared because the market for the product already exist.

By exchanging ideas, suggestions and or complaints, we have the potential to create and improve the quality of life for ourselves and still maintain the pride of financial independence that we so rightfully deserve.

Furthermore, after having discussions and conversations with several of my colleagues it has become ever more increasingly important that this network support group communicate and unite to correct and improve some of the disabling systems that are in place that were meant to mean support. Such as, for beginners, I think that it's totally ludicrous of the amount of time endured to establish financial support in many of these cases when practically all cases are already being back with the necessary paper work such as medical records, applications and any and all legal documents required. It is even more disturbing of the fact that the majority of these funds being requested are not those of gifts and or charity but from moneys that were payroll deduction contributions into this fund specifically for this purpose.

Collectively, when you think about it, disabled people are directly responsible for a major portion of the financial infusion into the nations economies. The dollar amounts being poured into local economies do not come with an option, they represent "must have" situations which in return establishes a constant cash transaction. Not only that, they are responsible for high end technical job demands that stimulate the market by requiring medical fields, schools, and equipment manufacturing jobs to be needed. It doesn't simply stop there. Pharmaceutical companies and distributors profit well, transportation companies constantly advertise for drivers and the marketers peddle their wares to the public.

Now in return these positions usually require relocating people with families which will require individual housing, more schools, grocers and etc.., and etc.., and etc.

In my short time served in my new position it has become increasingly aware to me that most people with physical challenges are content to quietly go away to a corner in the room and stay hidden, like it's an embarrassment to continue to be a part of society. To those of you I say, "WRONG!!!" You're challenged, it happened to you, get over it. It's not like you had a choice in the matter. How many people do you know that'll wake up one morning and say; "well I guess I'll go out and get myself disabled, today?" Give me a break!!! You have nothing to be ashamed of. Disabilities are un-bias and can strike any one from all walks of life at anytime.

I offer this one small suggestion and or proposal to you, start by registering to vote and then exercising your privilege. Then write your state officials and let your voice be heard. Establish local support groups in your vicinity and seek out people who need help or can help you. Let's make some noise.

When you consider the challenged person, it's not just limited to people it wheelchairs but should include blindness, the hearing impaired, American veterans and the senior citizens of this country.

Imagine there for a moment that everyone with a physical challenge (within reason), took the initiative and or incentive to spend a couple hours a day in the local thoroughfares for incidentals like shopping, paying bills or even just enjoying nature. Now, imagine the impact this action would have on things that are ignored or taken for granted in the everyday walk of life, such as; rush hour traffic, the local infrastructure, the speed and quality of service, I think by now you should be getting my meaning. Then imagine, if this event happened on a Monday, every Monday, at the same time everywhere all around the world. Do you imagine that this event would get anyone's attention? Well, I for one most certainly do.

From what I can see the problem is in part, is that when there is a spokesperson for the cause, it usually only gets worldwide media attention if that person is a celebrity or just a high profile case. Even then the message is only receive with a purely sympathetic ear and once again is soon discarded. In isolated cases some charity donations might even pour in and then it's right back to the closet as usual. Once again it only serves as a token recognition.

To the ordinary Jane or John Doe, upon viewing the type of reception that is giving to these high profile cases, then they have to feel devastated. It's a feeling of emptiness and loneliness because you have to feel that you have no forum to operate on. I suggest that it's time to make a change. Nothing is expected to be corrected overnight but it is very important to make a beginning or nothing ever will be.

These suggestions are in no way to plan a freedom march but are in respect to that almighty dollar bill that everyone covenants so much, and since we are responsible for spending our share then we should demand to be treated like we deserve.

Therefore, I strongly suggest that this position not be compromised.

Also, keep in mind that with each person with a challenge comes an immediate love one, be it a spouse, relative or friend who shares into the day to day obligations and or responsibilities that goes alone with trying to make a quality of life, thus, at least doubling the numbers when it comes to supporters for trying to correct and understand the plight of the disabled person. You might also be surprised at the large numbers of caretakers who often become frustrated when trying to deal with a non-working system that are willing to be staunch supporters and or sympathizers to this cause.

Remember, we helped build this system, too, therefore we should be included and not excluded. There's power in numbers.

CHAPTER NINE
HEROES AND HEROINES

This section is particularly important to me because it identifies, acknowledges and praise a special group of individuals whom I personally admire for their exploits. These people have withstood the battle of insurmountable odds and often endured a lot personal sacrifice without regret or remorse for the struggles they have seen. To call these people honorable would not be a strong enough word to pay homage to the tribute that they so rightfully deserve. In my eyes this people have earned the right to share that mythical god-like status of "HEROES and HEROINES".

Every time things don't quite go your way you probably sit there and moan about how bad you've got it. You might even be under some delusion that somehow life might even suppose to be fair.

It's so often you hear about situations where someone lost money in the stock market so they went on a shooting rampage and eventually was gunned down by the police. Romeo and Juliet lived out a suicide pact because they could not have the love they wanted. It's been well recorded and documented through out history that greater tragedies have been carried out for lesser reasons.

The people in this section are classified in two categories; (1) those who can't do anything about it but do and (2) those who can do something about it and do.

You're stripped of your lives and everything that you have come to know and all you are left to deal with is what's inside of you. At some point in life all of us become faced with obstacles and situations that we are forced to face and must try to conquer or endure, but when you are already aware of the fate ahead of you and you face it irregardless of the consequences, then to me you are a hero.

Short comings in any form are pretty difficult to overcome but we've been doing it since birth, crossing barriers, facing obstacles and fighting the odds. The situation changes slightly though when you've learned to overcome something and received it as acceptance and now must disregard all that you have grown to know and convince your mind to learn it all over again only this time a different way.

Now there's a lot of types of physical challenges; there's blindness, hearing impaired, speech impaired, physical and the main one that we all share, mental.

But all jokes aside, these people that I've met and come to know stand out in front of the crowd for two reasons; one because they're in a wheelchair and two because they're special. To give you a mental picture, I'm talking about people like Christopher Reeves.

With most other challenges there are remaining some other sense's that can be developed or functions that can compensate or over-compensate to make up for the one's that's been lost. In these peoples case all the senses and functions have been lost and the only functions left to work with is the mind and the heart.

It's not bad enough that you'll never again have the freedom to pick and choose your own direction or you'll never again feel the sand at the beach between your toes. And you know those nature walks, well, hold on to them and cherish those memories deeply.

Sometimes when it's real hot outside or you get horny and it didn't work out a cold shower would always be available to come to the rescue. I know that you understand how relaxing and entertaining that nice hot water in the spa or Jacuzzi can be. But one thing for sure, at least, you'll have feelings and sensitivity enough to be able to determine whether or not the temperature setting is right for you.

You also, even lose those birth given human rights, like the one to a little bit of privacy and something as basic as the ability to wipe your own butt after a good constitution is now gone. Say for instance you're on a family outing, or even worst there was a home invasion, it must be a helpless feeling not to be able to at least try and protect your family and yourself.

Then there's sex. I don't care if you're a man, women, boy, girl, or all of the above, if you've ever had this experience then you know what I'm talking about here and if you haven't then somewhere in your body or mind is dying for the opportunity just to get that chance. Yes, I know life is not all about sex but a large portion of it is while the rest is consumed with money. It's really hard to tell which is the most dominant, but I'd be willing to lay odds that it's sex.

But there's still some bigger issues involved here, let's say you've got some kids; can you see yourself not being able to tuck them in and kiss them good night. Can you imagine yourself being right there and not being able to catch your own child when you see them about to fall. When that kid needs a hug, who's going to hug your child today? Not being able to play catch with little Nickolas. Catching Ernestine when see runs to jump into your arms simply because she's just glad to see you. Just think, teaching your kids to ride a bike, helping them to be able to blow out the candles on that birthday cake, and laying on the floor underneath the Christmas tree and being unable to help them unwrap all the presents. That's a lot to ask from a person, and if that's not enough to drive you crazy yet, then there's more.

You've got a spouse or a loved one, I mean one that stayed by you because all the rest have already gone by now even for the ones who didn't even have quiet as severe of an injury. But let's say yours stayed, all those times when you made love in the rain, the candlelight dinners on the floor in front of the fire place, and the playful wrestling while showering together has now all been traded in for therapeutic sessions, cleaning of bedpans and losing a quality of life.

And if you think for one minute that this person is not already feeling guilty for merely existing and feeling like a burden to someone else and to society then buddy, you're wrong.

This person has got to live everyday knowing that there still remains human desires and functions that must be fulfilled and realizing the fact that they are no longer able to satisfy that need. To make a long story short, even though your wife stayed with you, you've got to be unselfish enough to know that she needs to be sexual fulfilled and know in your heart and your mind that she's out there doing it, and there's nothing that you can do about it but accept it.

I'm just touching on the top of a few issues here. There's bound to be plenty more that I don't know about, some pretty stupid and probably some much more severe. And we all know through out both history and personal experiences that a many of a people have given it all up and cashed in the chips at the window for way less of a reason.

These people have my utmost respect and admiration.

These folk unselfishly maintain a sense of respect for life and continue to try and still be a contributor to a world and a society that is no longer jest for them. That's one heck of a sacrifice to make I'd say.

I've taken special precautions and pains before to deliberately not mention certain individuals by name but on this occasion I will reverse that decision so that everyone may know who these very special people are. Their names are: Barbara Sansbury, Van Fuller, and last but not least, Lucile (my sister) and Jimmy Hall (my brother-in-law).

Like everyone else in the world, these people had their own lives to live, complete with their own set of problems, too. But, unlike everyone else in the world these people still were able to find time for compassion and caring for their fellow man.

It's not really important that they just so happened to be related to the people they actually helped. I'm not even entertaining the idea that this somehow was the glue that held this bond together. It was not unusual for me to wake up during the night and eavesdrop into the cries and moaning of others with tears falling down their face like rain. These people cried their hearts out because nearly everyday someone was being discarded by a friend a family member or by a loved one right at the very time when they would be needing them the most.

Excuses ran rampant in social circles as people often offered explanations of not being in a position to help or simply just not wanting to get involved. But the true defining element involved here was the willingness and commitment to make a sacrifice.

I hold special high regards for Lucile and Jimmy because, in my time of despair they were right there from the beginning and have remained one of the only constants in my life to this point besides my kids.

Hardly a day would go by that I could wake up without looking into one if not both of their face. It may not now seem like such a big deal, but when each day you live you are physically and financially unable to care for yourself, then believe me, it's a big deal.

Lucile somehow would manage to be there at the hospital through three separate feeding sessions a day and most of my therapy programs while still juggling a job, church participation, taking care of a house and a husband. Between the daily commutes it was amazing that there was room for any time to sleep.

These other two ladies whom I previously mentioned may have been there to be with someone else at the time but their dedication and loyalty was equally as persistent and bore just as much respect and recognition.

This cycle took on much more than just being there physically, there was a lot of physiological and financial repercussion involved, too.

You see, it takes pretty remarkable energy and courage to look at someone close to you laying in a hospital bed, resembling nothing of their former self, and you're trying to support them emotionally and convince them that everything is going to be alright when you're having a pretty hard time believing it yourself. You've got to suppress your own feelings and emotions because you're playing the role of the pillow of support. That's got to be hard and incredible.

Financially, now, that's the mother of all jokes. If you eliminate hospital bills and surrounding medical cost, and if you eliminate household and child care cost and solely consider the pending cost of intangible incidentals, then you're going to be in debt up to your neck. (No punned intended.)

For starters, none of your clothing will fit anymore because of the sudden changes in ones physical limitations, which means a new temporary wardrobe. This wardrobe is due to change at least three times depending on the stages and/or conditioning of ones progress. And remember, that does include shoes. Then there's the assertive devices and health aides that the insurance companies wont pay for that can easily topple into thousands of dollars. This is a progressive thing, too. Your pillar of support has to eat also with no mercy being shown from the cashier at all the high priced eating establishments surrounding a place of mercy. Their there like vultures, just waiting for something to die. In no way can you leave out the daily parking fees and the expense of gas from all the necessary commuting. But the insult to the injury is, if you're from out of town, man, that's a whole new can of worms. There's the hotel or apartment fees, the baby sitting or house sitting fees (depending on which type of arrangement your situation requires), and you've got an additional traveling expense because no one is in a position to completely walk away from his or her job.

Then there's Jimmy. He's a pretty unique individual in himself. In many ways he sort of found himself in a situation requiring understanding, sympathy and most of all a great degree of tolerance.

When you take the time to look at things from his perspective he was being asked to give of his personal time and quiet a bit of financial compensation. You'll also need to consider the sacrifice of time and devotion being taken away from their home and marriage during this period.

Fortunately, for this relationship he is the one that cooks and prepare the meals but still, it's not much fun when you're always eating alone.

He'd often come and visit with me after church and remained supportive through out my stay in the hospital. Never, at any time did he show any signs of annoyance, regrets or retreat.

This support structure that I received from these two people would continue even after my discharge from the hospital and through out my therapy process. The really amazing part is though, that this compassion was not just limited to me but it also included my immediate family at the time and even spilled over to other people in the hospital who were hurdling the same or similar obstacles as myself.

My outpatient therapy sessions were generally three days a week with scattered doctor appointments and social service appointments alone the way. The required traveling time and expenses must have been horrendous coupled with the monetary contributions and support made to my then wife.

If there were any hardships endured during this time you'd never know it because their business was never made public display. And you know it had to be hard on them because it was hard on me, especially now that this family had assumed the responsibility for two.

Once you take in consideration, that by this time, how all of those so called friends, the family members and the chosen loved ones no longer can find time for you in their life, then truly you can admire and appreciate the spectacle of this event.

For a very long time there things would only always seem to get worst. The only path in the future was the road down.

After months of going through this pain of trials and tribulations I eventually lost my home with no place to stay and not enough money to do it with.

Un-be-knowing to me, before I could work out a solution or come up with an alternate plan of action the groundwork for a very important set of plans had already taken place behind the scenes.

When all other attempts had failed as the time expired I learned that Lucile and Jimmy had already set aside a place in their minds and in their home to receive me along with my family.

You've got to understand that surely this action on their parts was met with a great sigh of relief for it served as a temporary solution to an immediate problem for which there was no answer. But at the same time, for me, it was a fall of pride and a constant reminder of just how drastic this change in life was for me to be.

This change in residents meant changes in lifestyles for not just me and my family but for them and theirs. We're talking about at least one year to this date of going out of your way just to help somebody else.

Imagine taking your last bit of private domain and turning it into a public space. In essence that's what happened. It means, now you don't have the freedom to walk around the house with your draws on, no more making love on the couch and most of all no longer having the sanctuary of a place to retreat to when you need to escape from the rest of the world.

Not only that, there were ever increasing demands on transportation requirements now that the distances between locations had so vastly changed. There were great demands on personality conflicts and uncertainties of the future. And irregardless, of what type of obstacle would arise these people would never utter a negative thought, all they would do is try a little harder or try a little longer to come up with and find a workable solution.

Sometimes when I look back and think about the way things have been, then I realize that these two people have been through just as much carnage and suffering as I have.

Since this time my wife and her child have gone, but I'm still here. The good thing about it is that now, some of the tensions and pressures have eased up a bit but the bad thing is that I'm still here.

Hopefully this wont last too much longer. It's not that it has anything to do with them on a personal set of levels, it's just that

I've still got my own pride, dignity and respect that must be upheld.

Basically, this is a bunch of regular folk, middle aged, not rich and not self righteous and domineering. To me, a bunch of passive, who believe in God; works hard everyday, and believes everything will eventually work out alright.

Still, the commitment, the dedications and the sacrifices are a lot to give up and/or ask for anyone to do, but these people do it un-waveringly and without reservations.

In no way do I attempt to include myself with this find group of people, several times upon numerous occasions I've searched my heart, my mind and my soul, just to see if I could ever take their place. And in being true to myself, the answer is that I really don't know. I don't know if I'd ever have that much courage or strength but, I do know that there is a whole lot of other people out there who don't. That is the difference that makes this so special.

I suppose that it's one of those things where you'll have to cross that bridge when you get to it.

This thing, as far as I was concerned proved to me that there are still good people out there into the world. It's like there has been a restoration in faith, a belief in mankind, and some hope into the survival of our future.

You may not know who the heroes are but when you see one you'll be glad that they're there. It's not just a myth.

CHAPTER TEN
ALL CREATED EQUAL

Imagine if you will, a place, a. people, a time, where individuality is promoted equally as much as the unity. Imagine if we really felt in our hearts the things that we say with our mouths when others are watching. Imagine if there were no need for the Equal Rights Amendment or an Affirmative Action Plan. Pretty scary, huh? Darn straight!, and you know why? Because we'd all be physically challenged.

That would probably scare the pants off you as much then as you are afraid now, afraid of the unknown. It's found to be easier to fault or blame another as a mask to admit ones own phobias. "I don't like him because he's black.", "They work for nothing and take all the jobs.", "They destroy everything they touch." Go ahead and add a few of your own. See, if you could continue then you're guilty, too.

Being physically challenged forces one to face his or hers fears, to accept reality and be better prepared to deal with the future.

When was the last time you've ever just stopped and had a conversation with a stranger?, or have offered assistance to someone in need without being asked or paid?

We all first came in here with an attitude, carrying around that same old everyday pre-conceived ignorance that's gained in life through the teachings of what we like to refer to as the civilized man. No one had any idea of who the person was next to them or where they came from. No one knew the religious affiliations of one another or political preference. We didn't even know each others name and no one was trying to find out. Yes, we are products of our society, we are the civilized man.

Pretty ludicrous idea to access to rationality that something good can come from a bad situation. Maybe the truth of the whole matter is that it takes the dramatics to help bring attention to the point. Never-the-less, there's a lesson to be learned here, but unfortunately, it's going to continue to go on unheeded. It's happened that way through out eternity. Perhaps that's also attribute to the fact that the survival rates for the physically challenged people was not very high in the past. Fortunately, over the last few years those numbers have increased dramatically.

Once having personally experienced a life threatening loss it becomes easier to know and share the hearts of another who grieves the same. People quaintly say in times of despair "I know how you must feel!" I suppose it's good etiquette or something but for the most part they have no idea what it's like.

We, people with physical challenges, have in common the loss of a life's long work and dream. We share a new and uncertain future, and we share an interruption in an already short life cycle that can never be replaced. Therefore, when support is shared it's not that it's the politically correct thing to do, it's because you have experienced the days, the weeks or the months of living with pain. So when your heart goes out to one another it's not out of sympathy but out of respect.

Respect; now this is perhaps the operative word. A lack of respect makes it easy to be bias or degrading to another individual but this is only because there is no appreciation or understanding for the efforts and energy required to reach this point. Sharing the knowledge of the amount of fight required to regain basic motor functions in life such as eating makes understanding the struggles of another more acceptable.

The respect factor in itself not only has a lasting amount of effect on the individuals involved but has the power to transcend through spouses, families and friends. For example; if someone is supportive and kind to a love one of yours, out of gratitude and support of your loved one you'll be more adapted to return services in kind. Now, couple that with the fact that the one offering the support has the same or similar situation, you now have sympathy and support for that person and their families and vise versa. It's the trickle down effect. Even more important, race or gender has no role here.

This reminds me of a scenario that occurred when I was transferred to the Shepherd Spinal Center. I was assigned to a ward that contained four beds and three of them were already occupied prior to my arrival. The center insisted on having wards to provide camaraderie and to help prevent depression during these disastrous times.

The other three occupants just so happened to be of my same race and even though we all suffered a bit of depression still, we would reach out and try to help each other where ever possible. Such as, the guy who could stand would reach the things up high that were out of the range of the people in chairs, and the person with the working hands would open the doors or soda tops, and etc.

Nobody, wanted to be here but we had to learn to make the best out of a bad situation.

Eventually, we lost one of our roommates that was discharged to go home, the big day that we all waited so desperately for. But in the interim, it left a vacant bed in our ward.

Well, after a few days passed we received another roommate, a guy from rural central Georgia. It became easily apparent early in his stay there that he had not had much associations with people outside his race and was definitely not pleased about having to share any space there.

Any attempts to communicate were quickly shunned off and he was always reluctant to participant in any group activities unless the people involved were of his own race.

As time went on we came to accept it as such, but these actions could not sway any further attempts to touch base.

Such as life would have it, early one morning when the entire hospital and staff are waking up and preparing to begin another day, this gentleman was feeling kind of poorly. Or should I say worst than usual. Well, when he returned from the washroom he made an attempt to transfer from his chair to the bed, just like he had so many times before. This time since he was weaker than usual he fell over to the floor between the chair and the bed.

No one really knew in the beginning what had happened to him because he always kept his section of the room closed off from the view of the rest. All I know is that there came this faint cry-out for help.

For certain, all of us together weren't physically able to help him. Since I happened to be a bit more mobile than the rest of my roommates, I called for assistance's 'stat', a term that I picked up from working in a hospital during my college years.

The response was immediate. Doctors, nurses and therapist dropped whatever they were doing and came running in from all sorts of angles. It was a very impressive and emotional time.

After assistance had been administered and things returned to something resembling normal, he called my name and told me thanks. I nearly had a cardiac, myself, for that had been the most words he had said to me since his arrival and besides I didn't even think he knew my name. To me that moment was worth more than gold.

The next series of events really shocked the pants off me, he then proceeded to call his friends and family members on the phone and describe to them the series of events that had happened earlier that day and how his new friend had come to his aide. He began speaking and talking with the rest of the guys in the ward that very same day.

Later on during the day when visiting hours came around when his family and friends came to visit him, they too, for the very first time started to speak to us and show some sign of concern about our well being. It's pretty unfortunate that it always have to take something drastic to happen first, as if, things in life aren't already bad enough.

There seems to be only two times in our life that we have any sense, when we are children and when we are dying. All the rest of the time we seem to be totally ignorant as people and that's because we're either taught it or because we've learned it.

A many hours have been spent at the negotiation tables, numerous documents have been signed and plenty of lives loss senselessly on the battle fields just trying to reach the point that we are now. It's down right embarrassing how much can be gained through something simple as a physical challenge when we exist in a world full of scholars, technology and civilized man.

It's not to be assumed that challenged people stilled don't have prejudices or harbor some sentiment for racism, however, if they do, it takes a seat on the back burner. Cumulatively, we have come to learn how to reject stereotyping and respect diversity. I suppose that's because of something as simple as the love of life.

CHAPTER ELEVEN
IT'S ACCEPTABLE CONT'D

Good evening and welcome back to another segment of "IT'S ACCEPTABLE", brought to you once again from those fine folk of 1-800-DIS-ABLE.

We'd like to hope that you enjoyed and had the opportunity to experience some of the subject matters discussed in our last series and we sincerely hope that you are able to once again enjoy this program equally as much.

Remember, if you'd like a repeat performance or have any questions regarding previously discussed materials, then please keep in mind, it is made available to you by simply thumbing back a few pages until you've reached the desired areas of your choice.

We'd also like to thank our sponsor for bringing to you this fine educational program.

* * *

This period we will be sharing our spotlight with a member of "First Hand Experience", a person who is an elite member of the group of physically challenged people from all around the world. This person received his training on the spot, without the use of visual aides, text books or talk show host. He will be bringing to us today his past and present day experiences, viewpoints and ideas in order to hopefully better serve you the individual and the community.

We'd also like to remind you once again to keep in mind, that some of the materials may seem controversial or offensive in nature but the views and opinions discussed in this story do solely reflect those of the writer.

* * *

All right, so now without any further undo delays, let's give a warm welcome to our distinguished guess, an astute individual and a member of "First Hand Experience",...how about a nice round of applause for Mr. Hand D. Capp.

Host: "Welcome Mr. Capp, first of all I'd like to say that it's an honor and a privilege to have you here and to commend you and your fellow co-hearts, for all the fine work you've done in your neighborhoods and throughout the communities. Let's get right down to the point!,...what is your assessment of people with challenges and the job market? Do you find it more difficult now than before to be an active participant in society?"

Guess: "Thanks for having me here, Dick. In answer to your question, the answer is no! After an injury and recovery quiet a number of people are able to return to work without much difficulties and for the ones who are not able to return or find suitable employment, well, we like to attribute their contributions to the fact that the vacancy which they leave behind helps keep open a viable job market thus allowing someone else the chance to work. Besides, if all else fails, then we become comedians.

Host: Mr. Capp, I've noticed that you don't often see many challenged homeless people around, why do you think that is? Is there an agency that aides in this area?

Guess: Why, no Dick. Unlike most homeless people who are forced to sleep in cardboard boxes that are usually left behind to liter the streets and make eye sore the community, people in wheelchairs that are forced to sleep outside have homes that are mobile. Get it, "mobile home!"

Host: Mr. Capp, in your opinion, why do physically challenged people seem to fit in so well in society that they practically go around unnoticed?

Guess: That's easy Dick, we're the same people that we were before becoming injured. Most people were model citizens from the start, besides, could you imagine a person in a wheelchair being involved in a roll-by shooting or better yet, a guy on crutches shoplifting? How fast is he going to run? No, these people lived with character and respect in the past and continue to do so now.

Host: Okay, Mr. Capp, I need to wrap this thing up but I'll give you the last few minutes to share with our guest some of the advantages you've found since becoming physically challenged.

Guess: There's just so many that I really don't know where to start, but right off the top of my head; well, I no longer have to worry about the price of gas. OPEC can do anything they want to but my mileage remains the same. Then there's never having to hurry. Wherever you go or whatever you do people are always saying, "don't hurry, just take your time.", and you best believe me, I do. What, you think they want to make themselves liable for a lawsuit or something? And I'd like to add one more thing before I go and that's with a crutch you'll always have assess to a weapon and if you're a short person you can immediately add three to four feet to your reach. I mean like turn the lights off and on from half way across the room. I could just go on and on here.

Host: Sorry Mr. Capp we're out of time here so that's going to do it for this part of the show so that we may return to our regular viewing audience, you know, it's time to pay some bills. But Mr. Capp, anytime you're in the area feel free to stop by and bring more enlightening inf. our way. How about another warm round of applause's, ladies and gentlemen, for Mr. Hand D. Capp!!!

* * *

So people come home tired and exhausted from work but still their days can not come to an end, and all those other little chores to do, pick up the kids from school, stop at the dry cleaners, do a little grocery shopping and the preparations for tomorrow. And even though your favorite movie is coming on tonight you dare not chance staying up and watching it because it's a week night. You know, early to bed, early to rise. Well, you definitely need to rise early because the traffic is so heavy in that area and there's always at least one accident or so it seems. But if that's not enough to make your milk curdle, the weatherman predicts snow in the forecast.

Poor soul, you have my deepest sympathy!, for I too, used to play by those rules. But today it's a whole new ballgame and I make up the rules as I go.

Instead of grudging in the mornings when the alarm clock goes off I simply hit the snooze button, pull the covers over my head and then I'm back off to dreamland. If I'm expected to do something and don't get around to it or simply just don't want to do it then I reach for my bag full of excuses. When I do decide to get up and spend a couple of hours a day on the computer my work is done and then its back off to watch "Judge Judy." But today I like especially, it's my favorite day of the week for it's the time to watch for the mailman, because it's payday.

* * *

Did you know; that you have now been granted with the gift of "available excuses anytime"? That's right!, at your convince, whenever you need out of a situation you now have an excuse.

Take for instances, someone wants to borrow money from you, well, you don't have to feel obligated to comply with their wishes because you're on a fixed income and probably don't have a job.

Or maybe, someone wants to come over for a visit or request your company to go somewhere. No problem, just reach right down in your bag of excuses and come up with any one you so desire.

This old bag of excuses is not available at your local department stores and you can't order it up on television. The only way to obtain this gift is by becoming disabled. That's right, ladies and gentlemen, disabled.

So rush right out today and become disabled so you, too, can get your own bag of available excuses.

They work extremely well especially, when vocational rehabilitation and workman's compensation are trying to send you back to work.

Remember, taxes and shipping charges may vary in your area.

* * *

So you've lost your house because your benefit money didn't come in soon enough and you have no place to stay. So you can't find another housing because you're on a fixed income and you can't qualify for today's going rates. So what, that your credit ratings have been shot all to heck because you weren't able to pay your bills on time.

Well, don't despair, all is not lost, there's several ways you can possibly remedy this little problem. First, you can take up residency in your local homeless shelter, eat free meals at the neighborhood church and bank roll your benefit checks. Or you can apply for government housing through a chartered agency and received low or discounted rates of rent depending on your specific needs. But almost always, you can now bed down with any one of your newly acquired friends or family members that you are sure to attract now that you have that guaranteed monthly government check coming in on time through rain, snow, sleet or shine each and every month.

With the security of knowing that you definitely have money coming in, people will flock from miles around just to kiss your butt and try to suck a few dollars out you. (Well, at least the week before and the week after the mailman runs.) But hay!, it beats the heck out of being homeless.

* * *

Well, that brings us to the end of another chapter of "IT'S ACCEPTABLE". As always it's been a pleasure to once again be able to serve you and keep you all informed. I know personally, that a lot of the views and opinions expressed would probably not ordinarily come into the boundaries of your minds or if by chance they did you'd probably feel unsure or even uncomfortable about the notion. But trust me on this one; it's okay, and you know why?...because... "IT'S ACCEPTABLE."

You've got to be able to find the positives, you've got to be able to separate yourself from the situation and become able to find the humor in life, otherwise, you're going to miss the beauty in life.

CHAPTER TWELVE
COUCH POTATO

The time is July, the year is 2000. For the first time in my life I'll be taking a pro-active stand and actively be participating in an annual citywide competition, the Peachtree Road Race.

No, it's not a misprint. It's true that I'm paralyzed, quadriplegic to be exact and this is not a special division contest to be involved in. Also, let it be noted, in no way is this entry intended to be a placed victory but merely a victory to mark the progress of my one year anniversary since my injury. It is intended to shed more awareness to the flight and cause of people with physical challenges, and last but not least, it is intended to be my way of thanking and bringing recognition to the wonderful and professional people on the staff of the Dekalb Medical Center and the Shepherd Spinal Clinic who were very instrumental in the state of me and others like me to be able to recuperate and regain control of our lives.

For a little bit of history here, this is a 6.2 mile race which is notorious for it's hills. It's ran every 4th of July with professional grade participants from around the world. Last year, (that'll be 1999 for those of you who can't do the math), my level of participation was limited to sitting outside in front of the Shepherd Center and viewing this race from the comfort of my wheelchair.

Then I made a vow to actively seek a role in the upcoming event. My therapist felt it was their appointed duty to accept and hold me to this challenge and let it be known, neither one of us will be the first to say quit.

But for this I will say, my final position in the race will not be first, but I will definitely not be last. If last place positioning comes down to me and a little old lady about ninety-five years old, then you best believe, I'm tripping her up. So a word to the wise, you better not let your mama enter. Nah, just kidding.

Okay, now before we go any further let's do a little bit of background here. First of all, I'm forty-seven years old and was the picture of health before my injury. Well, maybe not the picture of health but could do two-hundred push-ups and two-hundred sit-ups a day religiously. Although, being somewhat of a couch potato, I'd get home from work and suck down a few suds, smoke cigarettes and play on my play station until early morning light. Then get up and do it all over again. Sounds familiar?

All right, so it's "D" day and for all practical purposes as far as I was concerned the "D" stood for done. After my injury it used to be possible for me to work up a sweat just trying to relay a mental message from my brain to any given part of my body.

In no way did it have anything to do with me being lazy because I used every ounce of strength available at my disposal. But since my muscles had been deactivated from my nervous system for a while they were no longer a friend to me, they became a foe.

For all intense of purposes the first initial reaction was to bounce back up and shake off this injury as soon as possible. That later proved to be easier said than done. The practice of expending exuberant amounts of energy for an all but seemingly useless cause became so demanding and strenuous that laying around all day and doing nothing became a much more satisfying solution, even though everyone involved knew that was not a practical answer or best course of action to take.

While laying up in bed one night and sleeping like a baby, (I mean I had my favorite teddy bear with me and everything), well, the fire alarm went off. No problem, this picture of instructions in my mind says to hop right up, get in my chair and be outside in just a few minutes. A sound game plan it was, too. One small problem; I didn't have enough strength to lift the cover's off me.

How do you spell panic? No problem, stay cool, let's go to game plan number two; wait until someone comes to get you.

You could not imagine the speed at which your heart rate increases each time a second ticks off the clock. The sounds of motion and rumbling can be heard out in the halls as you once again began to calm down. Then the sound comes closer and closer so you sigh with relief as it has got to be your turn. Next, they pass you by and go to the room next door. All right, the next one will be for me you ponder while you start to gnaw on your bottom lip but still it turns out not to be. Don't worry though, three times the charm as you are swept away to safety in the arms of a heroic caretaker. By this time instead of being grateful for being rescued your fears have turned to anger and you're hotter than any fire could have turned out to be.

It all turned out to be a false alarm. Now I'm doubly pissed. I was nearly the last evacuee, my peaceful sleep was disturbed for no reason and most important of all they left my teddy bear in the room.

The following morning, guess who couldn't wait to get back into the gym? Starting with a bunch of ranging motions performed nearly ninety percent by the therapist the program was up and running. These people were committed and would dish out as much punishment as you were able to tolerate. This group of aides would later on become known as physical "terrorist".

Time appeared to pass quickly and before long I was able to make some moves of my own. Progress shifted from bed to wheelchair and now to crutches. Hopefully soon I will be able to abandon them also.

Testing has covered areas such as physiological and physical. It gave me great pleasure to have a negative check in areas such as A.I.D.S., prostate, heart trouble, diabetes, high blood pressure and sickle cell anemia. What a start! It's been so long since there was a beer in my system that drinking has become a thing of the past. And my training program is so vigorous that my smoking habits have reduced nearly fifty percent. Once my physical strength has regained it's normal potential it will no longer be a laughing matter to hear me say, "I'm a picture of health."

"Good-bye" couch potato, "so- long" beer belly. The next six pack I get will be the muscular development around my waist. Since joining the gym my visits there are at least three times a week and we have purchased several pieces of equipment for use at home.

This turned out to be one of those things you always wanted to do but never got the chance. Well now I've got the chance. Funny how these things work out.

UPDATE:

Well, I did succeed in participating in the Peachtree Road Race, however, I was physically unable to complete the full 6.2 miles due to equipment failure.

I did succeed in bringing public awareness, inspiring other patients at the Shepherd Spinal Center to continue to work hard, and fulfilling a personal sense of accomplishment.

All in all, it was great. I was awarded a shirt that was won by a successful competitor who wanted to do something special and show some recognition for the effort put forward.

Thanks, again Gwen, my hat goes off to you.

Things went so great that I'm recruiting to bring a larger contingency of participants to next years event.

CHAPTER THIRTEEN
HERCULES

It sure was great when feelings and sensations began to return to parts of my body that had been dormant through out this whole ordeal. There were so many areas of concern until it was practically impossible to determine, if preferable, just which area(s) would hold the highest priority. Of course, it was very important that everything regained it's natural function, or as much as possible, but it would definitely be a lie to say that list didn't include that priceless heirloom; the family jewels.

One day during a question and answering section with one of my many doctors I took the liberty to voice my concerns for which I was somewhat disturbed. After a series of several questions and a few test it wasn't long before he was able to lay waste to the worst of my fears and reassure me that everything was going to be all right. Although, while being very elated from the words of the good news that I had just received, in all reality I knew that it would still be a very long time before they would be able to go out and take that long awaited road test. That was quiet all right with me though, just the mere fact of knowing that they would be there when I needed them would be enough satisfaction for me, for now. Besides, at this point my strength was pretty much non-existent and there were numerous other physical challenges that demanded my immediate attention at this particular time.

The mind is a terrible thing, it'll set it's own agenda on desires and relinquish memories of tranquility at it's own disposal. Even if you try to consume yourself with other activities as to take your thoughts in a different direction, sometimes nothing seems to work. If in the event you are fortunate enough to avoid the mental mood swings you still have to be aware of and try to overcome the physical ones. These are sometimes not so easy to avoid and cold showers can only work for just so long.

This thing has been brewing about to a boiling point for a very long time now. All systems are ready and set to go. I don't know about anybody else but it's a big event for me. My first road test in months and I'm ready to go solo. The desires are eating away at me from the inside. The anticipation is driving me wild with rage; it's been a long time, you know. The mind is swimming around in a pool of lust just thinking about past experiences and days gone bye. I'm in a big hurry to get this thing on so I can know one more time what the feeling is like. I don't know if I want to do it right now because the feeling might leave and I want this feeling to last forever. What if this thing don't work right? What if I get tired? What if, what if, what if? What if this is a big disappointment, it could be devastating and embarrassing to both me and the girl? Maybe, I should just wait for a while.

Well, I just had to find the answers for myself and it's true that they definitely weren't going to come to me in a bottle, so I set out to seek the help of a professional, I went to find me the comfort of a woman.

In order to accomplish the task of the mission which now I was embarked upon I stopped at one of the local establishments of entertainment, one I'd frequent on several occasions before. But this time it was different, it was purely therapeutic.

The ambiance of this place in itself immediately had a positive impact as my body began to respond and many of my questions and fears soon started to dissipate. The smorgasbord type selection of such fine morsels of flesh made it hard to make up my mind. There were tall ones, short ones, fat ones and skinny ones. And they say that it's hell on earth. Yeah, it was hell all right; hell trying to make up my mind.

After a couple of drinks and some light conversation with a petite delicacy, we quietly careened off to a secluded spot so we could be all alone. Admittedly though, I was somewhat caught off guard by the actions of my therapist when she reached inside my pants to examine my family jewels, although, the soldier stood proud as a peacock and I was more than pleased to see him rise to the occasion.

One thing lead to the next and to the next and to the next and pretty darn soon the sparks of passion had blazed into a full raging fire. It got so hot in there until the sprinkler system activated.

From this point on I was completely satisfied that whatever body functions would be remaining lacking and for whatever reason they would chose to do so, that without a doubt, I had the best one back again. This made me very happy. But little to my surprise did I know that there was yet a couple of secrets to be revealed.

It wasn't long before the first secret decided to reveal itself and to my wandering surprise I think it made me happier than it did her. See, due to the nature of this injury it causes a prolonged ejaculation which in turn means that you have to have sex longer before you are able to reach an orgasm. I think that I can honestly say I don't think that there are too many people alive today that would complain about that one.

Once being deeply embellished into a seductive wrestling match for a considerable amount of time the rage grew with great intensity. Between the sweat covered pretzel wrapped bodies that were held together by deeply embedded finger nails it was hard to tell where one body end and the next one began. One thing was for certain though, this thing was about to come to a head. There was just no way in the world that anything could hold back this much tension and this much pressure once they've combined, besides, this is what I came here for and I was not about to be denied.

It's here, it's time!, this thing is going to blow!! Inside me there's this rumbling and churning and movement that's tugging away at the very core of my soul and leaving me weak from trying to hold back the force but at the same time it left me ecstatic at anticipating it's release. Can't fight it off anymore, this thing is going to erupt with all the fury and fire of the Mt.

Saint Helen's volcano in the 80's, and my target is well set and primed and ready to receive me.

But wait!!! Just as this eruption is about to reach it's climatic point of release something else takes place triggering yet another set of reactions. Cataclysmic like, with the volcano about to erupt a series of earthquakes are now set in motion through out my entire body.

I've never experienced this kind of a feeling before. " It's some kind of a side effect from my injury, isn't it?", I silently questioned myself. Somewhere in the back of my mind I knew it was just too good to be true. Something's happening. Something always happens!

Suddenly, and without any control I let out a scream. "Aughhhh!!!", and then she screamed, too. "What in the world is happening here", I'm wondering to myself as our clutch on each other seems to have tightened through the violent and vicious set of involuntary twitches and grinds. One might have thought that our wet and sweat covered bodies may have brushed up against an electrical outlet or something.

Then it seemed as if it was coming to an end and our holds on each other began to subside. Now it was time to recuperate and catch our breath when it struck back once more with just as much fury and rage as it had the first time. This force was so violent that it had the strength of ten ordinary men. We ranged out one more time, "aughhh!!!", as if our parts in a chorus was due in a song being sung by a choir. Here, was born the beginning of a new word: "SPORGASM".

Our drained bodies laid entangled still desiring to nurture the last ounce of passion from this fruit, when without any warning, one more bombshell was still about to be released. With this last and horrendous eruption the screams that cried out must have sound more like a desperate plea for help rather than a joy of pleasure as someone knocked on the door to make certain that everything was all right.

There was not enough left between the two of us to answer so they knocked again.

Finally, after being sexually satisfied to the point of total exhaustion, I mustered up enough strength to squeak out a reply.

Then I looked over to my partner and observed her lifeless body that I lay next to. I held my breath as to make certain that she was still breathing. In her face with eyes that was still closed she wore this sheepish smile of a grin. Then she reached down with her hands and raised my loins and with a girlish tone of voice she said, "you're my hero."

A "sporgasm" can best be described as a series of involuntary muscle spasms which can and usually do last anywhere from three to five minutes combined with an orgasm which triggers multiple reactions from ones partner. You won't find this word in any dictionary but believe me, it does exist.

Our therapy sections still continue to this day but without the aide of the local establishment. We've kind of moved our appointments to private quarters that we now share together. She seems to keep murmuring some silly nonsense about making a honest woman out of her but that's another story, this story remains about "sporgasms", just another one of the benefits that goes along with disabilities or in this case abilities.

CHAPTER FOURTEEN
LETTER TO SALLY JESSY RAPHAEL

Dear Sally,

I've watched your show on numerous occasion and viewed it with great pleasure. Of all the other talk show host that I have watched, I've noticed that your forum has always upheld a high moral standards without causing ridicule or embarrassment to your guess. You and your staff seem to be genuinely concerned with helping other people and/or resolving issues. It is for this reason I have chose you and come to you now.

Well, you see Sally, I need help.

About one year ago I had the unfortunate pleasure of having an in home accident that resulted in a broken neck. Two vertebrae were destroyed, the C-3 and C-4 respectively, leaving me in a quadriplegic state, thus hindering me paralyzed from the neck down.

Fortunate, however though, my spinal cord injury was not a complete injury and with the help and blessings of "GOD", Dekalb Medical Center, and definitely the Shepherd Spinal Center, I have been able to recover most of my motor skills and begin to learn once again how to utilize their functions.

Although, it's been a long year, I figure at this pace it'll still take me at least another two years before I'll be about 80% healthy again, which will more than likely be my peak achievement. But for this I'm so thankful, many people are not fortunate enough to recover that far. That's the good news.

The bad news is that this injury has left my life in ruins that will very likely never be able to be repaired or replaced.

As devastating as something like this might seem at first knowledge, no one can truly began to imagine the chaos caused associated with this effect.

Not only has the risk of my health been compromised but it also resulted in the lost of my job at a time when finances are truly critical; the lost of friends and family members, at a time when the very core of your existence needs to be supported emotionally because you're down and out and feeling all alone; but there also came the lost of my home which is symbolic to being left alone side the road to die because now, you really don't have the security of a shelter to allow time to recover. Last but not least, there was the lost of my spouse, the one that vowed to be with you until death do you apart. You have no idea the type of mental anguish this effect does to destroy the hope and the will to continue living in a person who has just already lost everything worldly in his possession.

Sally, I've seen your shows, and you make things happen. What I need is not so much in help for me, I need help to help other people like me.

These are real life issues that not only affect me, but, there's got to be thousands of people out there like me. People need to be made aware of what travesties of inhumanity that really do occur in situations like this. People need to be made aware of the plight of the disabled. These people at one time or another were all viable contributors in society and now are being discarded like old debris.

I've found out from talking with other people in my category that for some reason or another they feel some sort of guilt for their situation or they are ashamed because of their physical deformities. Because of this feelings, these people sort of exclude themselves from society and vice versa and live the rest of their lives sheltered away or hidden in some kind of a closet, be it mental or physical. It kind of reminds me of a person that's been raped, they feel guilty when in all actuality they are the victims.

I'd like from you, to see a show done reflecting disabilities and the people that are effected. The whole world watches your show and has respect for you, therefore, more people can become aware of this problem and regard it as serious.

I'd like to know how to set up a foundation to aide or help subsidize these people when that are desperately at a time of need.

Right now, it's just a dream for me. I, too, was never really knowledgeable or concerned about these people until it affected me directly before I realized they even existed. I'm glad to be over my ignorance. I'm sure that I can make this thing work and try to restore some dignity and pride back to an already broken people.

Sally, please help me help somebody else.

Sincerely,
Eddie Burley

CHAPTER FOURTEEN A: UPDATE LETTER TO SALLY JESSY RAPHAEL

Some six months have passed since I wrote this letter. Unfortunately, neither she or her staff thought enough about our cause to address the issue and/or help bring public awareness to the focal point.

No one bothered to take the time and offered a letter of refusal or even acknowledge the fact that they received my letter. This is just another case in the fact of what I am saying. Physically challenged people seem to become invisible until it hits home.

I'm only left to attributed it to the fact that helping real people in need is not ratings gathering enough.

A copy of this update will be forwarded to the show.

I just thought that you should know, in case you are one of those Sally watchers who just might be shopping for another way to spend your quality viewing time.

Apparently, we are not commercial enough.

CHAPTER FIFTEEN
MY SHOES

I've got shoes and a fine pair of shoes they are. Actually, they're boots and not shoes at all, but I love them just the same. As a matter of a fact, they're my favorite pair of shoes.

A fine, sturdy, rugged looking pair of shoes they are. They are made of black genuine leather and are ankle high boots with an oil resistance and slip proof sole. They are really an impressive pair of shoes to look at and they feel great when I have them on my feet. I got these remarkable shoes at "Payless Shoe Store" for a purchasing price of thirty-three dollars and they are worth every cent of it, too.

Each time I'd wear these shoes I'd look good in them and they'd make me feel good. I could wear them with a pair of jeans and take on the persona of an outdoorsman, like hiking, hunting, lumberjack, and things of that nature. Other times while wearing them to work with my uniforms they'd exude such sharp and crisp outline to my already well defined masculine and intelligent physique until a captive audience would immediately be impressed when I'd walk into a room. There was hardly any occasion when they couldn't have found their way into my wardrobe, for instance, with calf length white socks rolled down to the top of the boot while wearing baggy short pants, my head rag and a pair of sunglasses, man, you ought to see the females heads turn when I strut my stuff. Yeah, they go for that bad boy image, and I must say, I look good when doing it, too. They are perfect, there's a fit for all occasions.

The more I think of it, I doubt if a time went by while wearing these shoes that someone didn't offer a compliment or make an inquiry about them. And that would always work well for me because I really do enjoy showing them off. These boots to me are my lucky shoes and it seems every time I wore them I always looked and felt good.

Funny thing about these shoes though, it also appeared that each time while wearing them something chaotic would occur just when I'd be looking and feeling my best with plans for just a simply day.

The first time that comes to mind was on a Friday; it had been a long and exhausting week at work when everyone involved busted their butt to make sure that all our challenges for the week would be accomplished prior to the weeks end. And everything was turning out right on target, we were ahead of schedule with nothing left to do this day but get paid and go home. Everyone felt good, we were excited, confident and laid back, just awaiting to come the end of the day.

All the job orders were completed for the day, the landscape crew was out cleaning up the property for the weekend, and we had a solid game plan laid out and devised for the weekend. It was around 3 o'clock in the afternoon with only two more hours remaining until quitting time.

It was very important that everything be as flawless as possible because the owner of the property was visiting town alone with representatives from the franchise that we were affiliated with to do an upcoming inspection.

It was a great opportunity as far as I was concerned to stand out and shine; blow my own horn; if you will, now that, at my disposal was the undivided attention of all the main and key players concerned. It presented itself as a great career opportunity and I was not going to be denied. Hey, I was even dressed the part, I mean, I was looking good, too, seeing as how I even wore my new boots to work for the very first time.

The clock was ticking down, the distinguished party had arrived, I made my rounds and met everyone and things were going according to plans. One thing we didn't plan on however, was for the landscaper who was applying the final finishing touch of pine straw to the property to drive his vehicle onto the grounds. As well as you can imagine, this did not turn out to be a very good idea.

Water now begins to spew from underneath the ground as the irrigation pipes gave away unto the weight of the truck. The situation probably wouldn't have had to be so bad only if it had been reported at the time of the incident, but no-o-o, no one was willing to accept responsibility so it went on un-noticed until; that's right, one of the owners stumbled across it at exactly a quarter 'til five.

The limelight was an all too familiar place for me and I was able to perform commendably. The usual routine, dig the hole, repair the line, restore the service and then finish the product as if nothing ever had happened. Not a problem.

As far as I was concerned though, there was a problem, one major problem, my favorite boots were now all covered with mud.

It took a couple of days of hard work, toil and labor to restore these shoes back to their luster. There was the scraping of mud, the washing and drying and then relentless hours of polishing, buffing, polishing and buffing. But the effort did not go all unheeded for soon the pride and glory was once again the shoe.

So time passed. In light of the last episode concerning my shoes I took the extra precaution to wear them back to work on selective occasions. Today was one of those days.

I could drag this story out with a bunch of small talk and irrelevant details, but the bottom line is my boots got screwed up again. It turned out to be just another classic case of SOS, just a different day.

This time it happened to be the guy's responsible for replacing the marquee sign. It didn't really matter much to me because all I knew is that the results were the same.

After cleaning my shoes this time, I had a protective interest and vowed never to wear them back again into a hostile environment that was not worthy of their presence. It was all so obvious to me that no one or anything else respected and appreciated my shoes with the same authority invested in me. So at this point I reserved all rights and occasions to wear these shoes solely for personal and casual entertainment only.

This was not to be the last of the memorial circumstances that these highly treasured shoes would have an impacting role in my life.

In this series of stories, I've talked about a little bit of everything except for the details as to how I actually broke my neck. Well, don't you want to know? Of course, you do!

Once upon a time, after carefully cleaning and treating my shoes I failed to put them back into their special storage space where they had been kept so many times before. Then morning came and it was time to prepare for the next day. June 1st, 1999, 12:01 am., I left the bed in a heated rush and headed for the shower when I stumbled over my beloved shoes in the dark and struck my head against the door jamb. What a way to start the day!.

It wasn't a big fall, it was just the angle of the fall. Fifteen pounds of pressure applied to the right area at the right time was all it took. And the rest, as we like to say, is history.

A few times after the incident I'd wear these shoes as part of my wardrobe just to show them off to the public. Actually because of their stylish forte they make a great conversation piece to say the least.

Once other people find out the history behind me and my shoes they often wonder why in the world would I still be in possession of such a shoe. And still there are some who admires my intestinal fortitude each time I demonstrate courage to wear these shoes again. Then there's always those who would question my sanity.

But that's when it all becomes very clear to me that they just don't understand, these poor lost and misguided souls have apparently never had the chance to experience true love before and even if by chance they have, then it must have been so long ago until they forgot what it must feel like.

These shoes have done more for me in the short time that we have been associated together than anyone or anything has ever done before. The accomplishments and gains that have come in this period probably will not outweigh a lifetime of success but it has definitely made a pretty impressive showing.

I find myself now, a man of quality and leisure. Because of these shoes, now afforded to me is the enviable position whereas, I have the power of choice and the luxury of time. With this new found freedom comes the comfort of living life to it's fullest extent and no longer being forced to commit to work just to live.

Lot's of people on the outside could look in and quickly say. "Gee!, what a price to pay.", but that would just be a cop-out because they've obviously never really had any convictions or directions of their own. But like the old saying goes, "Don't knock it if you ain't tried it."

I've still got a few more reasons, times and occasions that I wish to wear my lovely boots on, one being the Peachtree Road Race that I plan to participate in this summer. This will perhaps be their final official use and opportunity for the public to see. At the conclusion of this event my plans are to retire them and have them bronzed as a keepsake and memoriam to the evolution of the life that I have come to enjoy.

I love my shoes.

CHAPTER SIXTEEN
A BETTER VIEW

I had a little problem. There was this big decision to make. It all started out with this event, college spring break coming up. Everybody was going to be down for it. Me!, I'm trying to get my 'Mack' on, know what I'm saying. Well, this player come up and asked me to loan him two-hundred and fifty to pay his rent and he'd give it back to me in a couple of weeks 'cause he had lost his job but started another and it would be two weeks before he got paid but irregardless, the rent was due right now.

Now, 'shorty', was a friend of mine, so it ain't like it was no real issues about the papers and things 'cause we've been there together before and my man always came through, but this time it was different, we talking honeys, 'FUBU's', and champagne, all...night...long.

And I weighed and considered all the facts carefully with my head, which one?, now that's debatable.

Anyway, I stepped up to the plate and told 'shorty' the truth, I just didn't have the money, then I proceeded on to the college spring break.

I could have done something about it but I didn't cause I had to get my 'Mack' on, you know what I'm saying. Besides, shorty would understand.

So, when I got back I stopped in to check on shorty only to find out that he had been evicted.

When I ran into shorty I was like, how come you didn't holler at me when you needed a hand, you know I'd be there for you but 'shorty' just shook his head and walked away.

When I left there I was like, O.K., what's wrong with that fool?

Then later I realized that I had let down a friend and that the problem that I was having was me.

* * *

I had a little problem, you see, I lost my job today, so while I was on the way home trying to figure out what I was going to say to my wife and my family when I got there from the place that used to be my job for the last twenty years, I became so consumed into myself that I saw but I did not see that young fifteen year old girl while she was being raped by three men in that alley in broad daylight that I couldn't take enough time out of my life to yell stop or at the least call the police.

Later on that day when I got home and saw the event on the evening news as the commentator reached out for help from any witness's or the unidentified man who was seen possibly in the area to come forward and help, the thoughts that must have run through my mind were, "what a fool", "this guy must have really been an idiot", "how in the world could anybody have been so insensitive?"

Then I realized that this person was me!!!

* * *

I had a little problem. Today I bought this beautiful new ring, probably about three and a half karat diamond on a twenty-four karat gold nugget band for seven-hundred and fifty dollars. And I know that you're probably saying, "what do you mean about?", but see, I bought this thing off the streets in the hood and neither one of us are the real jewel experts and besides she won't know the difference and really won't care, cause all she'll know is that it's big and shinny and pretty.

So immediately, I hurried over to my girls house to give her this ring and ask her to be my bride but as I came down the hallway to reach her place the door came open and a guy walked out with a fifty dollar bill in his hand. She took the money, told him that she loved him and he walked away singing and whistling just as I did the night before. When she had told me that she needed fifty dollars I thought that she meant that she needed fifty dollars.

When I left there I was so heart broken, not only cause my girl was a hooker but the jeweler on the street had a "no exchange, no refund" policy that when this poor old tired homeless man approached me and asked if I could spare a buck I pushed him back and said, "I don't have any money to throw away."

A little further down the street I put my hand in my pocket for some reason or the other and I felt that ring. I took it out and looked at it one more time and then it occurred to me that I had just thrown away seven-hundred and fifty dollars on a dream but couldn't spare a buck for a man who was in need.

I knew then, that the problem was me.

* * *

I had a little problem. Today, I had a tragedy in my life where I sustained a major injury, went through financial ruins and eventually lost everything worldly in my possession. I seeked around both high and low with my hands reached out and searching for help only to find out that like me before everyone else was so much into themselves that they didn't have the time or care to stop and help somebody else.

Hungry, homeless and injured was I when this person saw me and stopped.

They gave me food, shelter and bandages to nurse my wounds until they healed and I then was off on my merry way.

I have no idea why I started to write this except that it sounded good to me but then after I could read it on paper I saw things that at first I did not see. The problems that I had before were just that, little problems, but it could have meant so much more somewhere else if I had only taken the time out to stop and help. The pitiful thing about it though, is it had to happen to me before I could see and if no one had stopped to help me then heaven knows where I would be. To this day I still can't believe that I was once so shallow and selfish.

I had a little problem, but now it's gone away, I know now that when I see people who need help that they really do.

CHAPTER SEVENTEEN
ILLUSIONS

The flexor muscles in my hand won't flex and my muscles that are suppose to extend won't extend. My ligaments are stiff and my joints won't bend. So you see me spending a couple of hours a day in front of the television playing video games, it don't mean that I'm having fun with nothing else to do, I'm learning to use my hands again and doing my exercise.

* * *

My body weight is one-hundred and fifty pounds. I have sixteen inch biceps and can do two-hundred push-ups, seventy-five chin-ups on the pull-up bar and can bench press upwards to two-hundred and fifty pounds. On the basketball court my average it twelve points a game with four rebounds. I spend numerous hours per week in the swimming pool and begin each day with two miles around the football track.

Because my body is committed to this chair it don't mean that I'm not healthy.

* * *

Okay, yeah, so sometimes it's true. I need help occasionally, be it emotional, financial or spiritual. When I've had a break-up with my loved one and there's no recourse in sight, I just need someone to talk to who will listen to my needs. And it's true that my money is not long enough to buy the car that I want so I have to borrow money from a bank to purchase it with. And yeah, it's true, that sometimes the burdens of the world gets to be a little bit more than I can bear and I have to seek guidance and divine intervention from a higher power, but all these things make me just like you.

Now, because my body is in this chair, that does not make me disabled. You see, disabled means that you can not do. Granted, I'm a bit different from you, but what I am is physically challenged. I may not do things the same as you and some things might take me a bit longer than you. And then there's going to be times when I'll fail completely at the things that I'll attempt to do. But that's okay, and you know why?, because with each failure comes another opportunity to succeed. It's a chance for me to get more exercise in. It helps to restore self esteem by promoting independence. And last but not least it assures individuality.

Don't think that I don't love you or appreciate your desire to be there for me, but just because I need help sometimes, it doesn't mean that I can't think for myself or decide what clothes I want to wear anymore or even make my own decisions in life without your aide.

I need you to help me by trying to understand that the things that I need help with are the things that I need, not the things that make you feel better. Although my life has somewhat changed, it is still my life and you can not live it for me.

Just because I need help sometimes, it don't mean that I'm helpless, I'm just like you.

* * *

Depression is usually the result of one of life's little traumatic experiences, i.e., marriages, divorce, births or deaths, that has the tendency to lead to alcoholism, that is usually socially unacceptable and has the capacity to lead to a traumatic experience that can cause a disability or handicap that can lead to depression that can lead to alcoholism that is usually socially acceptable.

* * *

I was as strong as an ox, both mentally and physically, or so I thought. I could carry all the weight of the world on my shoulders and solve almost any problem, no matter how difficult that it may have seemed. And pressure, it didn't phase me none, as a matter of a fact it excited me and pumped me up a little bit more.

I lived with two homes, two women and two jobs simultaneously so there was never any doubt that I was the man. I could fight off any foe irregardless of his physical stature and I could lift my own body weight.

With all the strengths that I possessed no one was allowed to get close to me, not even the ones that I allowed to be near. I maintained this protective coating, this mental wall, whereas, my weaknesses and vulnerable areas, if any existed, were not exposed to the world for public scrutiny.

These days my physical state is far weaker than in the past, but I've torn down all the mental walls and protective coatings and I'm exposing all my underbelly to the public through my writings because I've realized through my injury how to face my fears and that I don't need them now because I'm mentally stronger and better able to handle it.

* * *

I've become a connoisseur of fine collectibles, if you will, memorabilia with some great stories to tell. Although, each items monetary worth is slightly no more than dollar face value they do hold quiet a bit of sentimental pride.

These items consist of a pair of shoulder crutches that were left from a broken leg back in '89, running for a bus, trying to work on two jobs. Then there's a shoulder sling from a broken collar bone in '93, from a construction accident at a girlfriends store. In 1999, while recovering from a broken neck, and you know the details by now, I've compiled a neck brace and a wheelchair from when I was first able to get out of bed. Later, I gained a pair of wrist crutches and a pair of knee braces from learning how to walk all over again. And last but not least, there is this cane that I use to steady myself in my final stages of recovery.

Now, I know it may just seem like just a bunch of worthless junk to you, but,:

When I'm in a crowded place and want to get a seat, the crutches will come into play and then someone will get up and let me sit down. The arm sling is always available when you need to get out of work. The wheelchair and neck brace is important to bring sympathy from a judge or jury whenever you need to sue someone. And the cane, well, it just makes me look good.

So as you can see, cumulatively, all these items are priceless.

* * *

I've heard people talk about it, even though I've never really given it much thought. I've read about it, but still it seemed too ludicrous of an idea to conceive. People have said before that you're older than dirt and there's been stories told of people living for untold scores, but that can't be true. Then still, there is the one about reincarnation.

I fell and broke my neck and almost died. I could have died but it just so happened that I didn't. However, if I had, then I just would have been dead and gone, and after a few short memories all would have been forgotten.

Well, as it turned out I got a second chance at life, I was reincarnated into this person that lives from a chair. And although there has been some lost that I've sustained from one transformation to the other, the trade-off is, that now I have been given the gift of immortality through my written word. Now, I will live forever.

* * *

So what?!, I was born poor, black and in America. So what?!, I was raised on welfare and then graduated to food stamps. And it don't really matter at all that I was raised in a Baptist church and sung in the choir and later moved on to be a usher and then a Deacon.

Who really cares that my wife slept with the preacher? And is it your fault that we didn't make it?

Well, what about my children that were born out of wedlock? And what about the wives that I married and we didn't make it?

There's no remorse or sorrow in my heart for all the married women that I've slept with.

And, nobody pays the child support but me. And who really gives a darn, what you think?

Where was God when my sister got killed? And, nobody cared that I had lost my faith.

Then there was the times when everything in life was wrong, and then I had an accident and broke my neck.

So what?!, you think that I'm mad at the world. And, so what?!, in my life I've met this girl.

And, so what?!, that I've been changed all around, it don't mean that I don't love.

* * *

Sometimes when my I'm in a lazy mood, I'll use my chair to get around in. Then there's other times when I'm up and walking that I have to use the assestive devices such as leg braces or a crutch. Now because this might seem a bit uncomfortable to you and make you sad to see me this way, it don't mean that I'm not happy.

* * *

I've always been known as this person with a style
and character that was all my own.

To a lot of people my attitude
and demeanor was very easily known.
I was both loved and respected for the role I had to portray,
but nobody really knew me for the things that I wanted to say.
Then one day this terrible accident left me unable to be,
the person that everyone knew and the person they thought was me.
Now with time on my side I write about my joys and pains,
of playing in the sunshine and making love in the rain.
I let a few people read what I wrote and no one would say if it was good or bad,
but, I could tell by the looks on their faces that they were feeling kind of sad.
After this accident I became just a number when they thought that I had lost my will,
but, after they read my book they realize that I am a person still.

CHAPTER EIGHTEEN
WHY DID GOD GIVE UP ON ME?

You have no idea, how it feels to live inside of a shell. Unable to feel, to walk or even to kneel down and pray. You'd be there sometimes from day to day, just trying in some way to ask for forgiveness for all the wrong that you've ever done in life. And then, sometimes you wonder through your cries as your eyes fill with tears, what did I do to deserve all of this. Am I suppose to be getting something out of this? Is there a special meaning in all of this? Do you have a purpose for me?, you find yourself questioning God. Why has thou forsaken me? But to no avail.

Sometimes, living from this position just ain't so easy, it's like being sentenced to a life imprisonment of solitaire confinement. Do you have any idea of how afraid I felt?, being totally unable to defend myself, but, reserved with enough resolve to still fight back.

You don't know what it's like to see others run and play. All you can do is sit there and watch and rely on your memories to help fill in the voids. And after you've remembered so many times even the memories start to fade.

You don't know what it's like to be afraid. I was at a point mentally, physically and emotionally where this life didn't belong to me anymore. Too scared to live but even more afraid to die.

There could have been a quick and peaceful solution to all of this you think sometimes. Death could have easily come and wiped all the pain and suffering away. But that would have been too easy. And then sometimes you think of taking your own life. Somehow, you figure that some stupid miracle is going to happen where God mysteriously appears from the sky and restores everything back to the grand splendor that you enjoyed before. Or you may be so angry and defiant that you refuse to give in, no matter what the consequences. It's like a challenge to God, and making Him do His own dirty work. Otherwise there'd be something else to hold against you.

So what?, benevolent God, this is how you humble your subjects, by making them bow down to you and sing your praise., I thought to myself.

Is this suppose to be my just punishment for not carrying out the Glory to God?, for having the strength and charisma to do for myself. And whereas, it is told that thru your own doctrines and teaching that if I take one step then you'll take two. Well, isn't that pretty much suggestive that I should be self sufficient?

With all my doubts, disbeliefs and the things that I have done wrong, surely I have done more good that could outweigh my errors. But now I suppose that you're upset with me for questioning your authority.

So, God, why did you tell me that you'd be there for me, yet when I needed you, you were gone?

And, then, a period of silence passed.

When all of the self pity, the anger and the emotions were gone, the picture took on a whole new view. God didn't give up on me, I had His undivided attention, even if it was for only just a little time. For with the ways that I used to be able to touch people and help them alone the way, now, I'm able to do this thing some 100 times fold. And for all the hard times and pain and suffering that I have had to endure to reach this point, well, now I have been delivered from.

LAST
R.I.P. (THE BEGINNING OF THE END)

Nearly all of life's changes seem to be centered around pain of some sort. Although pain can be very discomforting at times it does not necessarily mean that it's such a bad thing. Pain is there to help serve as a reminder that we are still alive. Pain is there as a warning, a red flag if you will, to bring attention to an element in life that may need to be dealt with immediately. And pain can also be a way of letting one know that they are healing, for although it may seem very intense from the beginning you're able to measure how much improvement has been made by it's demise.

Sometimes when I sit back and think about the pains that I have suffered and the way things have changed in my life and take account of the way they could have been, somehow, it seems that I'm a much more better off person than one might have imagined could be.

The learning and experiencing stages have been so wonderful that sometimes it's like a dream come true. I've nearly perfected this being physically challenged thing down to a fine art and with a little more tweaking and turning in the right areas do someday hope to be used as a teaching guide. Imagine that, me a teacher!!!

Its funny, all the aspects of my life that I was uncomfortable with and would have changed if I could just became possible. Who'd a thought that you could actually get a second chance to start over in life without physically dying?

The mental evolution has been great because it allows me to be me and not have to slow my pace down just so that others might be able to keep up. Now, my views and opinions are free to remain my own without every "freaking" word being subject to political criticism or debate. It's all so simple, if you don't agree with me now, then all you have to do is put this book down. Of course, though, if you're made it this far, for all intense of purposes it's too late because you're almost finished now.

Yeah, it's true that sometimes I lone for the days of old and there's times when I wish I could do some of the things from the past like making a fist and slapping the "snot" out of someone, but hey, at forty-seven years of age I'm a bit too old for that now anyway. But boy was it fun. But then again, I often wish that I could still do some of the things that I was able to do at twenty years of age, too. You know, two women at one time and things like that but as you get older you couldn't do that anymore, even if you weren't so challenged. So that's life, you just kind of pick up the pieces and go on. That's where that healing pain comes in.

So therefore, these changes are not to be despaired. It's very often been said, "if only I knew then what I know now." Here I sit with this vast wealth of knowledge that was learned and retained from days gone by with the opportunity for a fresh start and a clean slate. You could look at the situation and say, "but damn, that means you've got to start all over again!"; while I'll look at it and say, "gladly, anytime!" We are always so quick to highlight the negatives in a situation that we sometimes forget to appreciate the positives.

All in all though, it kind of reminds me of that beautiful bird, your know the one that rose from the ashes, the "phoenix".

Here I was, just a mortal of a man with all the problems and worries of the world on my shoulders. People pulling and tugging at me from all sort of angles like I was something good to eat. They had me coming and going at such a pace 'til I'd meet myself at the door.

After starting with all the usual struggles in life to reach that "status quo", where it's already been predetermined or influenced that we should all strive to be, alas, I had made my place in the world. Stripped of all my individuality and thoughts just to become another head of livestock in the herd of society. With the aide of all the fine shepherds around to assist you it then became very easy to lose one's identity.

Off in a hurry to be such a good little sheep I could hardly wait in line for my turn to achieve as much education as I could from some of the finest schools in the ghetto in order to go out into the world and find a job that would begin the journey that was systematically already prepared for me. Just think about it, becoming educated to work! Seems like some sorts of a paradox to me; if one is so educated then why in the world would you want to find work? Anyway, I did all the right things; dedicated myself to work and service that would never be thanked or appreciated and discarded at the drop of a hat, to getting into a heck of a lot of debt just trying to survive and eventually settling down with a family or three thus compounding the problem. The irony of this is, I had to get an education to do this?! Gee!, thanks. This is probably the type of a situation that the term “educated fool” refers to. Right about now if you find yourself thinking “that sounds like me”, then join the club. None-the-less, now it was official, I had joined society and become another member of the human rat race. Interestingly enough, somehow, through all that educated physco-babble I had succeeded in convincing myself that I was actually enjoying it too, at least for a while there, anyway.

I was making so much money out there at minimum wages that I’d end up owing the Internal Revenue Service money it seems every year for taxes but somehow there would not be enough moneys left for me to survive on. Go figure! Good thing all those fine banks and good people from the credit card companies were available to come to my aide or I just can’t imagine how in the world I would have made it. With the help of my new buddies now I was able to realize and appreciate some of the finer things in life that I really enjoyed and worked so hard for, nothing much, just a little groceries every now and then, a place to live without roaches and a couple of pairs of draws. Nothing much.

Something was wrong though. Even with all this help prices for everything constantly increased and I’d still end up owing the Internal Revenue Service. Not only that, by this time my new friends thought enough of me to take the liberties and include me on their mailing list and constantly remind me of how well I was doing at compiling a debt that I couldn't afford in the first place. They even thought enough of me to the point whereas they occasionally picked up the telephone and call me personally just to see how well I was doing.

At this point "red flags" started going off and I was able to recognize the signs of pending troubles ahead.

Of course, naturally, since being well educated I started taking full advantage of all the words of wisdom from the wise, "son, what you need, you need to get yourself some dependents and some deductions". "You know, you might actually be on to something there", or so I thought. It seemed like a great idea and so I did. Besides, there was this one little gal I'd had my eyes on for a while.

Two very important lessons I soon learned but not without an expensive cost was when you purchase a product that the most important parts of the package are the instructions and the consumer warning labels. To this day I'm a true believer that if you read these papers first that you'll probably change your mind about the purchase.

That one room efficiency bachelor pad that I live in was no longer large enough for the two of us and all her shoes not to mention the fact it was not proper and fitting enough to seriously entertain a woman, especially, one with a kid already. Did I happen to mention that I was doing drugs at the time?

Of course we eventually had to purchase more furniture, more groceries, more clothing and soon a car. Well now a car, hey, that's another story in it's self with tax, tags, insurance, gas, repairs, you name it.

So what?, I'm now in three times more debt than when I originally started, it's an investment into my future and besides there'll be tax deductions to write off this year even though it is just June.

Wasn't long after before that investment proved to be about as bad as the idea. It didn't turn out all bad though, for all my troubles and steadily rising debt, I did get two things from this new ordeal: (1) the birth of a beautiful first son, and (2) the right to pay child support.

Gee!, thanks. Darn!, warning labels. Why do they always put them in the box behind the product instead of before the freaking things.

Right about now, I'm thinking, "what the heck did I go to school for."

All right, so there's no time to cry over spilled milk (literally speaking), you just pick yourself up by the bootstraps, put your nose to the grindstone and keep on trucking. There goes that physco-babble again. Is there an echo in here?

So, I retooled myself. Went out and got more education, got myself a better job, made more money, child support payments went up, my tax bracket increased and so did my taxes. Did I happen to mention that now I was the proud father of a second son?

Well, if at first you don't succeed, then try, try again. That expression must have been coined by a wine-o trying to hustle up his next drink.

Finally, and another three kids later some retribution began to come my way. My two oldest sons had now come of age, there was only three child support payments a month now going out of my pay, the mortgage payments increased and I still owed the Internal Revenue Service.

But by this point I was feeling pretty good about myself because there was only ten more years of payments due.

My ex's all loved me though. If ever I was sick or hurt they wouldn't hesitate to come and see about me as to make sure I didn't miss any days off work. I was working like hell while they kept up with the soap operas. I used public transportation to get around while they each had new cars. Their furniture was new and mine came from the "second hand" stores. But I was a good man, just ask them, as they stood pack to run off any and all newcomers who might be threatening their piece of the pie.

Remembering back, it was always a childhood dream of mine to be able to retire at the ripe old age of thirty-five, and I came darn close to making it a time or two. So having to settle for forty-seven, well, that ain't too bad either; I'll take it, cause luck must be a lady tonight. Tonight I broke my neck. This is probably one of the first times I've ever wanted to say, "thank you, Jesus."

My initial reaction to this was to bounce back and get back up as soon as possible irregardless to what capacity I would be in so that I could continue the role that I was playing. And then one day it hit me, like a pop upside the head the way granny used to do and I had a little talk with myself in which I said, "self, sit yourself down."

It had come to me like a thief in the night that I had been playing that role for so long until I was actually believing all that educated physco-babble hype myself. The truth is, my dues have already been paid to society, my mark has already been made on the world and in essence I have nothing else to prove. One year ago today, I was working two full time jobs and trying to decide whether to pay the phone bill or the light bill next month. And as ironic as it may seem, every time I decided not to pay the phone bill, my job would call. Now ordinarily that wouldn't be such a big deal. But since I was a manager, it was a big deal.

Then there were the staff meetings where I'd be ridiculed. If I couldn't control my small household budget at home then how could I control twenty-million dollars of someone else money. Things had gotten so bad, that when I took out the trash in the mornings, the trash men would throw it back at me.

Well, as I sit here overlooking the beach at Panama.

I've decided that no matter what my final level of recovery turns out to be, I'm going to be handicap for the rest of my life and I intend to enjoy each and every last moment of it. So when the world stopped spinning, I got off.

Yeah, for sure, there's quiet a few people that's going to be mad and upset with me for the directions and the actions that I choose, but the way I figure it is, hey, they'll get over it.

There used to be plenty of days of pain and torture when I'd have to get up early in the mornings and get ready for work. I'd be up so early sometimes in fact, that I could shake the rooster and pull the cover up on the sun as I headed out of the door.

And paydays used to always bring tears to my eyes 'cause no matter how impressive the dollar figures were on paper, didn't a thing belong to me. My finances were so low 'til I'd have to pull down my socks to see.

These are new days, they still bring a lot of pain, but somehow its a different pain. It's that pain you get in your side from laughing too hard when you've heard a funny joke. Laughter seems to frequent this place now more than ever before. I think in part it's because I get to listen at every one else now "moan and groan" about how hard it is to get up each and every morning for work whether you want to or not. Or maybe, it's the one about how there never seems to be enough money to go around.

These little mothers are working their fannies off and I'm enjoying every minute of it. They sometimes get mad at me and call me names like "cripple mautherf____", but that only makes me laugh even more as I calmly remind them that they're the ones who have to go to work, not me! That has such a sweet ring to it. Personally, I think they should bond together and start a support group called "M.A.D.A.M'S"—for Mad At Daddies About Money's.

As for my buddies at the Internal Revenue Service, well, yes I still owe them but at least now my funds are low enough to receive tax refunds each year which will be retained until the debt is paid in full. The best part is though, at this rate I won't be accumulating anymore debt with them, for a while anyway.

You probably thought that I didn't see that look in your eyes on that last paragraph, didn't you? And if you're reading this it means that I've made print which makes dollar signs in the bank. But before your eyes start to gleam and smile and you try to come after me for money, then heed this, I've already sold the rights to my first three books to an undisclosed buyer for a buck.

At this point I've come up with my own set of conventional wisdom; "you can avoid the rush; be the first in line, and you can kiss my butt right now."

I can feel that pain coming on again.

You know, people constantly try to talk to me about "God" and visiting the church with them on occasion, but unfortunately I just have to keep telling them "no." You see, I'm afraid that if I go there a miracle might happen and get me up out of this chair and I'll have to go back to work again.

If only I had any idea that things would have turned out like this, then, I probably would have broken my neck a long time ago.

Now, I can rest in peace!

Whereas, once I was blind, now I see. JOHNS 9:25.

www.ingramcontent.com/pod-product-compliance
Ingram Content Group UK Ltd.
Pitfield, Milton Keynes, MK11 3LW, UK
UKHW040016200726
13854UKWH00001B/228